GREAT CATCHERS OF THE MAJOR LEAGUES

Colorful profiles of ten men who made baseball history for their play behind the plate and at bat: Yogi Berra, Roy Campanella, Mickey Cochrane, Bill Dickey, Bill Freehan, Gabby Hartnett, Elston Howard, Ernie Lombardi, Tim McCarver, and Joe Torre.

GREAT CATCHERS OF THE MAJOR LEAGUES

by JACK ZANGER

Illustrated with photographs

j 927.96

RANDOM HOUSE • NEW YORK

To my father.

Little League Baseball is greatly pleased to join with Random House in the establishment of a Little League Library. It is our confident belief that the books thus provided will prove both entertaining and helpful for boys of Little League age and indeed for their parents and all who are Little Leaguers at heart.

This is one of a series of official Little League Library Books. Each has been read and approved at Little League Headquarters. We hope they will bring enjoyment and constructive values to all who may have the opportunity of reading them.

P J McGovern

President and Chairman of the Board
Little League Baseball, Incorporated

Contents

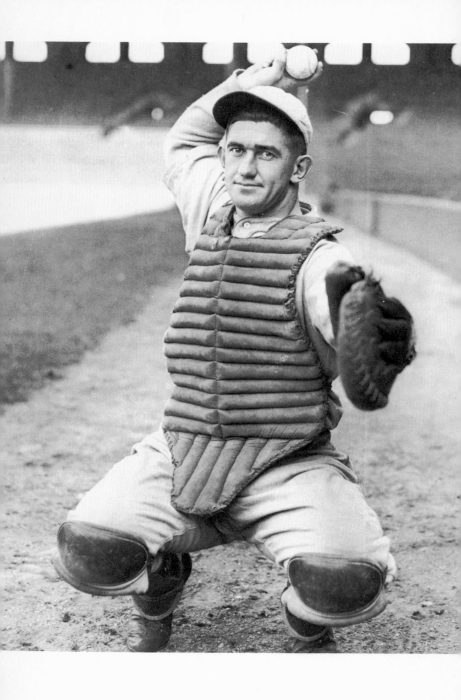

Introduction

The very nature of the way baseball is played practically dictates that catchers must be intelligent in their knowledge of the game. Catchers are often the extensions of their managers who have to sit and watch from the bench. The catcher is the only player on the field facing *all* the action. He can see things no one else can see. He can move the fielders around and plot strategy. As the man most tuned in to the pitcher, he is the first to know if the pitcher still has anything left or whether he should be taken out of the game. He can study the opposing hitters up close and spot tiny flaws in their style. By the very nature of his many responsibilities, the catcher has to possess baseball intelligence.

Further proof of this can be seen elsewhere. When the New York Mets joined the National League in the expansion movement of 1962, the first player they drafted was a catcher, Hobie Landrith. The explanation was that a team is only as strong as it is up the middle, and the middle begins with the catcher. When Jim Lonborg won twenty-two games in 1967 to pitch the Boston Red Sox to a pennant, he gave the credit to his catcher, Elston Howard, admitting he didn't realize the importance of a good catcher until Howard joined the Red Sox from the New York Yankees.

A roll call of some of the most important names in baseball history reveals that a fair share of them began their career as catchers. Connie Mack, the founder of one of baseball's oldest franchises, the Philadelphia Athletics, started as a catcher. So did Branch Rickey, who built dynasties with the St. Louis Cardinals and Brooklyn Dodgers, invented baseball's farm system and brought Jackie Robinson into the major leagues. Paul Richards, who became vice president and general manager of the Atlanta Braves in 1965, is regarded as one of the shrewdest brains in baseball. He spent his playing career as a catcher and then turned to managing.

Nor is it a coincidence that so many recent big-league managers are former catchers. The roster of managers in the 1960s with catching experience includes Ralph Houk, Al Lopez, Gil Hodges, Bobby Bragan, Herman Franks, Bob Scheffing and Wes Westrum. Of the catchers represented in this book, four of them became managers—Gabby Hartnett, Mickey Cochrane, Bill Dickey and Yogi Berra. Of the others, certainly Campanella would have been regarded as an outstanding managerial prospect if he had not been cut down by tragedy, and Elston Howard is still on the list of prospects. And who knows what the future may hold for such intelligent young leaders as Tim McCarver and Bill Freehan?

The catchers in this volume represent a cross-section of the top receivers of all time. In any listing of great catchers there would have to be Roger Bresnahan, Rick Ferrell, Frank Hayes, Walker Cooper, Mickey Owen and Josh Gibson, whose career was regrettably confined by prejudice to the Negro leagues; and there are many others, including 1968 rookie-of-the-year John Bench of the Cincinnati Reds. But the stories of the ten included in this book illustrate the talents, frailties, heroics and conflicts that have made all catchers so much a legend in the world of baseball.

GREAT CATCHERS OF THE MAJOR LEAGUES

Yogi Berra

The 1947 New York Yankees were a team of familiar faces. Strong faces. Handsome faces. Joe DiMaggio was on the club. So were Charley "King Kong" Keller, Tommy Henrich, Joe Page and Phil Rizzuto—all back from the war and ready to resume the Yankee dynasty.

Among such faces at the St. Petersburg, Florida training camp, homely, gnome-shaped Lawrence Peter Berra was sure to stand out. The stubby Berra was not exactly fashioned in the heroic Yankee mold. Moreover, he carried the curious nickname of "Yogi," which he had acquired in some forgotten sandlot game in bygone years. But if Yogi's looks, name and happy disposition were misleading, the Yankees soon learned that Berra earnestly pursued a major-league job. And though he may have looked ruffled in the famous Yankee pinstripes, Berra wanted desperately to make the New York squad.

Berra had been brought to spring training with

the mighty Yankees because of his reputation of swinging a powerful bat. But his credentials as a catcher were suspect. He possessed a strong throwing arm, but he scattered his throws. He had an ungainly, though muscular, body, which seemed ill-equipped for the fine art of defensive catching. There were other technical flaws which appeared impossible to correct.

Still, the Yankees liked the way he swung a bat. In the previous season, he had hit .314 for their farm club at Newark, collecting fifteen homers and fifty-nine runs-batted-in. Then, near the end of the season, he was brought up for his first look at Yankee Stadium. In his first at-bat in the historic ballpark, he blasted a home run. He hit another one the next day, and during the seven-game trial with the Yankees, he batted a robust .364. Surely, everyone reasoned, there had to be a place for the budding young slugger.

But finding a position for Berra would not be an easy task. A big-league catcher is one of the most responsible players on a ballclub. Playing the position requires many skills and permits few mistakes. On a team like the Yankees, with a tradition for winning, the demands were even greater. In Berra, they had a diamond in the rough. Though he was a catcher of pitifully limited experience, he had a way of hitting baseballs out of sight.

As the Yankees progressed through spring training of 1947, the happy young bumpkin began attracting almost as much attention by his comical actions as by his lusty clouts. He was likable and friendly, and funny things seemed to happen whenever he was around. His squat, stubby figure inspired many jokes from rival players, and his good-natured acceptance of the ribbing invited the bench-jockeys to grow even bolder. The writers, always on the hunt for someone to supply them with good copy, milled about the rookie. He just didn't look, act or sound like a Yankee, or even a major-leaguer.

Though perhaps the unkindest comments were made about Yogi's looks, there was a homely warmth written in the lines and crags of his face.

"You must be sick," an opposing player once yelled at him, "because nobody can look that bad and not be sick."

But Bucky Harris, the Yankee manager, said, "He's not ugly. He could become the most beautiful hitter in baseball."

Berra, hiding his sensitivity behind his busher's innocence, simply replied, "It don't matter what they say. All you have to do in this racket is hit the ball, and I never saw anybody hit with his face."

Berra had a fondness for reading comic books. One story told about him by his roommate in Newark, Bobby Brown, took place in 1946. Brown was studying to be a doctor, and often he stayed up late at night pouring over medical texts while Yogi thumbed through his comic books. One night, Yogi turned in early, leaving the future doctor engrossed in one of his books. Several hours later, he awoke to find Brown just shutting his book and preparing to turn out the lights. "How'd *your* book come out?" Yogi asked him.

Although Yogi had a limited education and his speech was garbled and often ungrammatical, he was anything but stupid. He had a native intelligence and he applied it to subjects that interested him. Baseball was the one which interested him the most, and in time he was to become one of the game's more astute thinkers. But he was not unaware of what people said about him. One day in the spring of 1947, a young fan approached Yogi for an autograph. Yogi obliged him, signing in the neat, careful style he used. "There," he said, "I'll bet you didn't think I could sign my name."

Yogi left a stronger imprint with his bat. He hit his way onto the Yankees and went north with the team. Harris wanted Yogi in the starting lineup somewhere. But letting him catch was risky. Harris finally decided to play him in right field. Yogi's outfield play left something to be desired, too, but he was less likely to hurt the club with his fielding out there. While he had the good baseball sense to throw to the right base, Yogi still wasn't accurate with his throws. In judging fly balls, he liked to study the flight of the ball first before committing himself. Often catchable balls fell for base hits.

In his rookie year with the Yankees, Yogi appeared in eighty-three games, dividing his playing time between right field and catcher. At the plate, he batted .280, smacked eleven homers and drove in fifty-four runs. There was no doubt he could hit big-league pitching. Then another facet of his amazing abilities became evident. Yogi was what baseball people call a successful "bad-ball" hitter. That is, he was adept at going after pitches outside the strike zone and stroking them for hits. Pitchers found it impossible to give him a base on balls, as Yogi swung lustily even at pitches that went over his head.

In games he caught, the base runners took great liberties at the expense of his scatter arm. He flung his throws high, wide and through Yankee fielders, and enemy benches taunted him. Yogi had scant opportunity to answer back—except with his bat —but there was one game where he gained a measure of revenge. A St. Louis Brown batter attempted to lay down a squeeze bunt to score a runner from third. Yogi pounced on the ball the second it hit the ground, swung around and tagged the batter almost before he left the batter's box, then dived headlong for the plate and put the tag on the runner coming in from third base. It was a rare unassisted double play by a catcher. Explaining the play afterward, Yogi said, "I just tagged everybody in sight, including the umpire."

The 1947 World Series between the Yankees and the Brooklyn Dodgers was a critical test for Yogi. The Dodgers were armed with an aggressive young

Right from the start of Yogi's rookie year, the Yankees knew they had a big-league hitter.

club of good base runners, led by fiery Jackie Robinson, who had topped the National League that season with twenty-nine stolen bases. Robinson often made good catchers look foolish.

The Yankees started Yogi behind the plate in the first two Series games, and Robinson ran the bases at will. As the other Dodgers followed Jackie's cue, Yogi was unable to cope with their antics on the base paths. His throwing grew more erratic and he became bewildered. Harris finally had to sit him down in the third game. When Berra was put back in the lineup, he was in right field.

Yogi's only distinction in the Series was the pinch-hit homer he made in the third game; it marked the first time a pinch-hitter ever had homered in a World Series. But the remainder of Yogi's batting record for the Series was dismal. He had an average of .158. But despite Berra's poor showing, the Yankees won the Series in six games.

Although the Yankees pondered Berra's fate during the off-season, they certainly did not consider trading him. They may have been unsure about his prospects as a big-league catcher, but they had no reservations about his hitting. His dumpy body concealed the fact that he really was an excellent athlete, with more speed and grace than met the eye. But on close watch, one could see that the secret to his hitting ability was in his tremendously strong wrists.

In 1948, Yogi played in 125 games with the Yankees. His catching improved slightly, but his hitting progressed rapidly. He batted a solid .305 and collected ten triples, fourteen homers and ninety-eight runs-batted-in. He was going after bad balls and getting good results, prompting Detroit Tiger pitcher Freddie Hutchinson to say, "He's a bad-ball hitter, all right. But don't ever throw him a good one."

In the spring of 1949, the Yankees made a move which was calculated to bring out the best in Berra as a catcher. They acquired Bill Dickey as a coach and assigned him to work closely with Yogi. Dickey had been an all-time great catcher with the Yankees. One of the first things Dickey did to remake

Berra in his own mold was to station him two feet closer to the plate. Yogi had been sitting back too far, giving runners that extra edge when they made their break for second base. Yogi also had a weakness catching low pitches, and Dickey taught him how to block them better. As for the throwing problem, Dickey could see there was nothing wrong with Berra's arm except for the direction of his throws, and the old pro schooled Yogi on how to get them away quickly and accurately. Dickey had a willing and adaptable pupil. When a writer asked Yogi about the progress he was making, he replied, "Bill is learning me all his experience."

In the next three years, Berra became the best catcher in the American League. He worked hard to absorb Dickey's teachings and he applied them on the playing field. He began cutting down base thieves with his new-found accuracy. He studied hitters' weaknesses and got to know what pitches to call for. In 1949, he played in his first All-Star Game, starting an unbroken string that lasted fourteen years. He played with self-assurance and won a reputation of coming through in the clutch. Even sagacious old Casey Stengel, who replaced Harris as manager, realized what Yogi meant to the Yankees. Stengel referred to Berra as "my assistant manager." Under Stengel and his "assistant" the New Yorkers made baseball history: the Yankees won five straight World Series.

But Berra's development was best reflected in the

Yogi nabs a pop foul off the bat of Cleveland's Sam Dente.

rapid climb of his batting average and home-run totals. In 1949, Yogi's average dropped to .277, but he clubbed twenty homers and knocked in ninety-one runs. The following year, he hit .322 with twenty-eight homers and 124 RBI's. In 1951, he hit .294 and collected twenty-seven homers and eighty-eight RBI's. For the 1951 season, Berra was named the Most Valuable Player in the American League. It was a dream come true for a young man who wanted to become a professional ballplayer.

Yogi's dream began back in St. Louis, where he was born on May 12, 1925. He grew up in a section of the city known as The Hill, which was heavily populated by families of Italian immigrants who had come to this country in the early 1900s. He also grew up during the years of The Depression, when much of America was going hungry and jobs were scarce. The Depression was no time and yet it was *the* time to be growing up, for it fortified youngsters of the era with a strong sense of values. These values were impressed on young Larry Berra and his three older brothers by their father, Peter, who had emigrated to the United States from Italy in 1913. Peter Berra got a job in a brickyard. Hard and honest work, the elder Berra believed, was the only measure of security a man could find, and he urged his sons to study hard in school and make something of themselves.

But all Larry wanted to do was play ball. Not just play ball, but to be a ballplayer. And his zest for playing games was matched by his reluctance for sitting in a classroom. By the time he was fourteen years old, Yogi left school and went to work. Peter Berra did everything he could to prevent it, but there was no stopping Larry once he had made up his mind. The jobs didn't matter, just as long as they permitted Yogi time to play ball. He even managed to squeeze in a game of catch on his lunch hour by gulping down a hero sandwich consisting of sliced bananas over which he spread a layer of mustard. Years later, the father recalled Yogi's boyhood days, "Run all the time. Never seen him home a minute. Play everywhere he go, in the park, in the street, anywhere."

Larry Berra and his neighbor, Joe Garagiola, whose father worked in the brickyards, too, played for a local American Legion team. In fact, Berra was assigned to the outfield because his pal, Garagiola, was a better catcher. One of Berra's teammates began calling him "Yogi" and the nickname caught on. Nobody remembers why, but as Garagiola said later, *"What else* could you call him?" A man named Leo Browne, who managed the Legion team, recommended both Yogi and Joe to the St. Louis Cardinals. Branch Rickey, who was one of the shrewdest men in baseball during his lifetime, looked them over and offered Garagiola a bonus of $500 to sign a contract. But Rickey's offer to Yogi was less than $500. Yogi refused to accept it. "I wanted the same as Joey got," he said, "so I said no."

There is reason to believe that Rickey knew what he was doing at the time. He was soon to leave the Cardinals and join the Brooklyn Dodgers, and those who knew him well believed he really wanted to sign Berra for his new club. Whatever Rickey's motives were, Yogi didn't wait around to find out. He signed a minor-league contract with the Yankees after Leo Browne persuaded them to give him a bonus of $500.

Peter Berra was not happy about the signing. He wanted his boys to amount to something. Yogi's older brothers all had good jobs, and the father wanted the same for Yogi. The brothers, too, had been obsessed by baseball, but in their cases, Peter Berra's will had prevailed. Now, the three brothers joined together and pleaded with their father to let Yogi have the chance they never had. Peter Berra relented. Yogi went off to Norfolk, Virginia to begin his professional baseball career in the summer of 1943.

World War II was already well underway and the United States forces would soon beckon the eighteen-year-old Yogi. But for the moment, he was a ballplayer earning $90 a month. This was considerably less than he made on his job as a helper on a Coca-Cola truck. But this was baseball.

Berra batted .253 in 111 games at Norfolk, giving the Yankees the opportunity to draw some early conclusions about him: he was as raw as they come as a catcher, but his occasional bursts of power stamped him as a prospect for the future. The future was still several years away, for the following year, Yogi entered the Navy. He was stationed for a while back in Norfolk and then assigned to a rocket boat which took him off to the war across the Atlantic, where he participated in the Normandy invasion.

When Yogi returned to the States, he was sent to the submarine base at New London, Connecticut. He was soon recruited for the baseball team there, but to his utter disappointment, found himself assigned a seat on the bench. The manager of the team, Jimmy Gleason, had been a major-league out-fielder, and he frankly doubted Yogi's claim that he was the property of the New York Yankees. But one afternoon, during a game in which Gleason had used up practically everyone else on his bench, he beckoned Yogi.

"Hey, you," Gleason growled, "you say you played ball. Take a stick and get up there and let me see what you can do."

Yogi took two strikes. Then he swung at a pitch far outside the strike zone and struck out to end the game. "A fine ball you hit at," snarled Gleason. "I thought you said the Yanks owned you."

"That's right, sir," said Yogi, "and I murder high, outside balls."

But the next time Gleason called on him, Yogi pumped one out of sight. He was in the starting lineup for good.

Yogi came out of the Navy in time for the 1946 season and was sent to the Yankees' top farm club at Newark. His stubby body had begun to harden and fill out now, and his outlook became more mature. He knew it was time for him to show people what he could do. Despite the long layoff from profes-sional ball, Yogi had an impressive season at New-ark and was called up by the Yankees when the In-ternational League concluded its schedule. Few may have realized it then, but Yogi was up to stay.

By the mid-1950s, Berra established himself as

the American League's dominant catcher. He followed up his MVP year of 1951 by winning the award twice more, in 1954 and 1955, thereby becoming one of a select group of ballplayers ever to win it as many as three times. Between 1952 and 1956, his average never went below .272. During this five-year period, he averaged twenty-seven home runs a year. He began stringing together enviable records as a receiver, too, but even more graphic were his day-in, day-out performances. He was doing things more by instinct now than anything else. In the 1953 World Series against the Dodgers, for example, he killed a budding rally by pouncing on two consecutive bunts and firing the ball down to third base to get the lead runner.

The World Series presents an entirely different aspect of Yogi's career. People always remember him as being at his best in Series play. But the fact is he didn't establish himself in this light until 1953. Up to then, his Series contributions were sporadic. But starting in 1953, Yogi began to collect clutch hits the way some youngsters collect bubble gum cards. The Yankees were winning pennants in the 1950s with monotonous regularity, and each fall became a World Series showcase for Berra. Among his more memorable exploits were the three home runs he hit off Don Newcombe of the Dodgers in

Berra played in a record seventy-five World Series games. But none was more exciting than Don Larsen's perfect game, which Yogi caught, in 1956. (N. Y. Daily News)

1956, one of them a grand-slam. In the seventh and deciding game, he belted two off the big Dodger righthander to wrap up the Series for the Yanks. As Yogi rounded third base after his second homer, he shouted to Newcombe, "That was a good pitch I hit, Newk." It was Berra's way of telling Newcombe that he had gone after a pitch outside the strike zone.

All together, Yogi played in fourteen World Series covering seventy-five games—both records. He compiled a batting average of .274 with twelve homers and thirty-nine runs-batted-in. It takes nine lines in the record book to tell the complete Berra story in World Series play.

In 1957, Yogi had his poorest season at the plate, hitting .251 with twenty-four homers and eighty-two RBI's. He wasn't yet ready for retirement, but he was beginning to show signs of his age. He was thirty-two years old now and he had begun wearing eyeglasses. He got his average up to .284 in 1959, but the following year he caught fewer games.

Yogi still had some clutch hits from time to time. One of them came during a doubleheader against the league-leading Detroit Tigers in 1961. Yogi didn't start the first game. But the game went into extra innings, so Berra was summoned as a pinch-hitter in the eleventh after the Yankees had loaded the bases. Tiger pitcher Hank Aguirre got the count to two-and-two on him and then Yogi lined a single over the third baseman's head to bring in the deciding run. "I just reached out and went with the pitch," he explained.

Finally, in 1963, he yielded the first-string catching job to Elston Howard. At the end of the campaign he retired with a lifetime batting average of .285 for eighteen seasons, with 358 homers and 1,430 runs-batted-in. As a catcher, he set records for most consecutive chances without making an error (950), most consecutive games without making an error (148), and most putouts by a catcher in league play (8,696).

In 1964, Yogi succeeded Ralph Houk as Yankee manager. But the team did not start out by playing up to expectations. Despite the fact that Yogi rallied the Yanks in the last month of the campaign to win the pennant, he was dismissed after the team's loss to the St. Louis Cardinals in the seventh game of the World Series. Some people blamed the firing on the fact that Yogi was too friendly with his former teammates, and that he could not hold command of the team. Whatever the reason, he was replaced by Johnny Keane, the Cardinal manager who had bested him in the Series. For the first time since 1946, Yogi was out of baseball.

But not for long. A month after his dismissal the baseball world was startled to read that the New York Mets had hired him as a player-coach. Yogi was reunited with his old boss and mentor, Casey Stengel. It didn't take him long to win over the new world of the young Met fans. He remained as a

(Top) *Berra, the Yankee manager, chats with John Keane before the 1964 Series. Later, Berra lost his job to Keane.* (Bottom) *Yogi's popularity is strong among youngsters.*

coach after Stengel was succeeded by Wes West-rum in 1966 and then by Gil Hodges in 1968.

Now, years after catching his last ballgame, Yogi remains the same friendly character he always was. Players still kid him and the fans still love him. Whether at home at Shea Stadium or on the road, his dumpy figure with the Number 8 on his back is a familiar sight in the first-base coaching box. All it takes to draw a cheer from the stands is for Yogi to go chasing a foul ball.

When one stops to think about it, nothing much has changed. He's still chasing after bad balls, one way or another.

Roy Campanella

Hoping to upset the Dodger pitcher's concentration, little Phil Rizzuto of the New York Yankees darted gingerly off third base, taking a daring lead in foul territory. Behind the plate, Brooklyn Dodger catcher Roy Campanella sat in his crouch like a Buddha, hanging out the sign for the next pitch before shifting into his receiving position. The Dodger pitcher nodded once and made his delivery. Campanella suddenly rifled the ball with a quick overhand flip to third base. Billy Cox planted the tag on Rizzuto, who slid back into the bag too late.

The Yankee shortstop picked himself out of the dust and, head down, walked back to the bench. Later, after the game, he said, "As long as I've been playing, that's the first time I was ever picked off third by a catcher. What an arm that guy has."

Rizzuto was talking about the young Roy Campanella, then in his second year with the Dodgers and playing in his first World Series. The year was 1949, just the beginning of Campy's fabulous career, but already baseball men agreed that he was destined to become one of the greatest catchers of all time. Something in Campanella's manner, something in the way he carried himself indicated greatness—from the very first day he came up to the big leagues.

That was in 1948, a year he began in the minors. Campanella was playing for the Dodgers' farm team at St. Paul, Minnesota, where he was hitting a hefty .325 with thirteen homers and thirty-nine runs-batted-in. Meanwhile, in Brooklyn, the Dodgers were slowly sinking from view. Although they had won a pennant in 1947, they were now fighting to stay out of last place. They were growing desperate and needed help.

On June 30, Campanella played both games of a night doubleheader at Toledo. He hit a home run, a double and a single. Afterward, as he wearily began pulling off his spikes in the Saints' locker room, Manager Walter Alston came up to him. "I've got news for you, Roy," Alston began. "Bad news for me, but good news for you. The Dodgers want you right now."

Two nights later, in the Dodgers' cozy quarters at Ebbets Field, Campanella put on uniform Number 39 for the first time and saw his name written into the starting lineup. In a game against the rival New York Giants, played before a packed house, Roy broke in with the kind of flourish that was to endear him permanently in the hearts of all Dodger

An expert technician in the field, Campanella tags out New York Giant Jack Harshman.

fans. He smashed a double and two singles and displayed the superb catching form that was to become his trademark. Even so, the Dodgers lost the game, dropping into last place.

Still, Campanella's emergence on the scene signaled a rise in Dodger fortunes, for he was to be the spark in five of their successful pennant drives. In his second game with the Dodgers, he collected two singles and a triple, and the following day, he hit his first two major-league home runs. He now had nine hits to show for his first twelve at-bats. When the team went to Philadelphia for a double-

header with the Phillies, Manager Leo Durocher
told him he would only have to catch one of the
games. Campanella's round face took on a look of
genuine hurt. "What's the matter," he asked, "did
I do something wrong?"

Campanella could do no wrong in Brooklyn. After
his impressive entrance into the majors, Roy took
hold as the Dodgers' Number 1 catcher for the remainder of the season. He batted .258 in eighty-
three games, with nine homers and forty-five RBI's.

The following year, 1949, he really began to establish himself. Campy's first full campaign in the
majors was a success all around. He helped put the
Dodgers into the World Series against the Yanks
with a .287 batting average, twenty-two homers
and eighty-two RBI's. Opposing teams soon learned
that his arm was just as dangerous a weapon as his
bat. Of the thirty-eight base runners who attempted to steal on him, twenty-three were thrown
out. The runners soon began to pay Campy the supreme compliment of not running on him at all.
When a writer approached him one day and casu-
ally mentioned that there was a conspicuous lack of
traffic on the base paths whenever Campanella was
catching, Roy laughed and said, "The fellows don't
run so much on me because they know I will throw.
I will throw because I always think a runner is going to go down. No matter who he is, whether he's a
slow runner or not, I keep reminding myself that he
might try it. I'm convinced you have to do that or

else you'll look up every once in a while and there he'll be, halfway down to second before you can do a thing about it."

Campanella was the premier catcher of his day. More than that, he was favorably compared to the greats of an earlier day—the Cochranes and the Dickeys. A catcher has to know how to "sit" properly, and Campy had model form. Despite his burly build, he was compact. He could get down low on his haunches, hang out the sign, shift into the receiving position, prop his glove up in front of his body and then present a perfectly stationary target for the pitcher. He never seemed to be out of position, and his movements were fluid and precise.

His arm was a miracle of swiftness and accuracy. With that snap overhand motion he had developed early in his career, he could whip a ball down to any base and put it right in the fielder's glove every time. And his ball was light as a feather to catch. In addition to everything else, he was excellent at handling pitchers. He seemed to possess a special intuition for knowing what a pitcher could do best in a given situation. In turn, the pitchers had complete faith in Campy's judgment and let him call the game.

In 1951, his third full year in the majors, Roy was voted the National League's Most Valuable Player after hitting .325, belting thirty-three homers and driving in 108 runs. The fact that he had to beat out Stan Musial for the honor made Campy's selec-

As a slugger, Campy set a home run record for catchers. Here he crosses the plate after smacking one against the New York Yankees.

tion all the more remarkable. He received 243 points, with eleven out of a possible twenty-four first-place votes, to Musial's total of 191 points. "It was really a very great honor," Roy said, deeply touched. "I never expected it. I sure didn't."

During the three-year span between 1949 and 1951, Roy reached a milestone never before achieved by any other catcher. He hit twenty or more home runs in each of three consecutive seasons. Only Gabby Hartnett had ever hit as many as twenty home runs in three different seasons, and he hadn't done it in consecutive campaigns. One Hartnett record, however, still eluded Campanella. That was the record number of thirty-seven homers Gabby had hit in 1930—a high mark for catchers.

Campanella bettered that mark in 1953. Although injuries had caused him to have his first slump in 1952, when he batted only .269, he came back the following season to achieve the greatest year in catching history. He hit a blistering .312 and established new records for catchers by hammering forty-one homers and driving in 142 runs. The combination of Campy's superlative hitting and catching enabled the Dodgers to capture another flag, and Roy was named the league's Most Valuable Player for the second time in his career.

The Dodgers of Campanella's era were consistently the most dangerous hitting team in the game. The lineup was packed with such distinguished sluggers as Duke Snider, Jackie Robinson, Gil Hodges and Carl Furillo, and boasted All-Star shortstop Pee Wee Reese and a pitching staff headed by Don Newcombe, Preacher Roe, Carl Erskine and Clem Labine. Yet even in such company, Campanella was singled out as the team's most dependable clutch hitter. Time and again, in game after game, season after season, Roy would come to the plate to provide the tying or the winning run. Inevitably, he would deliver the crucial blow.

There was another way in which Campy was valuable to the Dodgers. His jolly good nature kept the team loose and helped relieve the tension during the pressure days of a pennant race. He was amiable and friendly. Although Campanella was one of the first black stars in major-league baseball, he didn't take as militant a stand in the area of civil rights as, say, Jackie Robinson. He loved the game and could spend hours sitting around, talking of nothing but baseball and regaling his listeners with his repertoire of stories.

He was also a tireless, durable worker who prided himself on the fact that he had caught as many as three games in a single day when he played in the Negro leagues. His joy at finding himself playing in the majors perhaps was best summed up when he said, "This is where I want to be at all the time. The big leagues are the place to be."

In 1955, for an unprecedented third time, Roy again was the National League's Most Valuable Player. How could he help being chosen? He batted .318 and collected thirty-two homers and 107 RBI's. For the fifth time in seven years, he led league catchers in putouts and chances accepted. The Dodgers also set a precedent by winning their first World Series ever, taking the Yankees in seven games. Roy contributed two homers and a .259 batting average, but he made an even more significant contribution behind the plate. It was Roy who told Johnny Podres, the Dodgers' young, hard-throwing left-hander, to use his change-up against the Yankees. "It'll keep them off balance," he said, and he was proved right.

Podres won two games against the Yankees, including the seventh and deciding game. "Campy knows everything," said a grateful Podres.

But it was Tris Speaker, the great Hall of Fame outfielder of another generation who perhaps put Campanella into the best perspective. After watching Campy play several times, Speaker said of him, "Of all the men playing baseball today, the one they will talk about the most twenty or thirty years from now will be Campanella."

There is no simple way of telling how Roy Campanella reached the top, but his story began back on November 19, 1921, when he was born in Philadelphia, Pennsylvania, to an Italian father and a Negro mother. Right from the start, Roy realized that if he ever was going to amount to anything, he would have to depend on his own initiative and hard work. His father toiled as a seller of fruits and vegetables, and money was a scarce commodity around the Campanella household. Roy had neither the encouragement nor the opportunity to grow up lazy.

At age nine, he was earning twenty-five cents a day by helping his brother, Lawrence, deliver milk. The boys would rise at 2:30 every morning and finish the job in time to catch a little more sleep before going off to school at eight o'clock. This routine enabled Roy to play ball during all of his spare daylight hours.

By the time he joined his high school team, he had already attracted attention as a local sandlot player. He had grown rapidly and at the age of thirteen weighed 150 pounds. But high school ball wasn't enough for him. Roy also joined a semipro team known as the Nicetown Giants. Despite the fact that he was the youngest player on the team, he was one of the best hitters. His strong throwing arm made him a natural for catcher.

A couple of years later, the Bacharach Giants, a Negro professional team, offered Roy $25 to play for them on weekends. In those days, long before black players were admitted into organized ball, the only chance a Negro had to play professional baseball was with one of the Negro teams. When the Bacharach Giants were scheduled to play a Sunday game in New York, Roy wanted to go along with them, but he was afraid his mother would object. Mrs. Campanella told Roy he could go if he promised to attend church first on Sunday. Roy agreed.

The visit to New York opened the world even wider to the fifteen-year-old boy. During this trip he was approached by the Baltimore Elite Giants, of the Negro National League. As far as Roy was concerned, the Elite Giants were "the majors," and he readily accepted an offer to play for them at $60 a month. The year was 1937, and America was trying to ride out the sorrows of The Depression. Like many others, the Campanellas were doing all

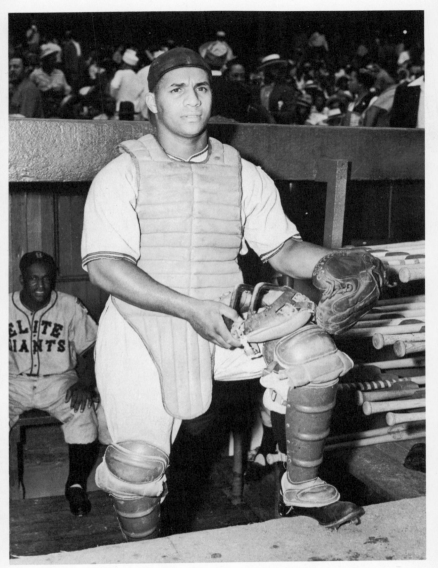

Campanella got his training in the Negro leagues, often catching doubleheaders. Once he caught four games in the same day.

they could to keep home and hearth together. For Campy there would be no going back to high school now; that was all behind him. Baseball would become his way of life—his only way of life.

Playing baseball in a Negro league provided none of the advantages or glamour of regular major-league baseball. The Negro players traveled constantly, stayed in dingy hotels, rode in steamy, dilapidated buses, and received little medical attention. The pay was low. Roy discovered that the only way to make any money was to play every day. "The fellow who played every day got the best salary," he said, looking back on it years later. So he played with all kinds of bruises and other hurts, and he played as many games as he could find to play.

He once managed to squeeze in four games in the same day. He caught a daytime doubleheader in Cincinnati, then sped to nearby Middletown, Ohio, where he caught a twi-night doubleheader. "I wasn't tired," he recalled. "I was young then and I didn't mind." He was now earning approximately $90 a month playing for the Elite Giants, but he actually spent little of the money since he sent most of it back to his mother in Philadelphia.

For the next eight years, Roy traveled the route of Negro baseball. After putting in a full season with the Elite Giants, he would literally follow the sun to the Caribbean and play winter ball in either Cuba or Puerto Rico. "I guess I played about two hundred ballgames a year," he once said. "There were about one hundred twenty-five in the Negro League and about seventy-five more in Puerto Rico. I usually played ball all but two weeks of the year."

He became one of the leading stars in Negro baseball, along with Josh Gibson and Satchel Paige. By the early 1940s he was earning as much as $3,000 a year. But Roy's real ambition was still unfulfilled. He longed to play in the white leagues, where baseball really counted and where he could test himself against the best players in the game. There was talk during these years of breaking down the barriers against Negroes in organized ball, but it was still just talk. U. S. 1587812

Then, in 1945, Roy played in a post-season exhibition game in Newark between a team of Negro All-Stars and a barnstorming group of major-leaguers. On the field, he met Charlie Dressen, a coach with the Brooklyn Dodgers. Dressen informed him that Branch Rickey, the president of the Dodgers, would like to see him in his office the next morning. When Roy got there, Rickey told the young catcher that he knew all about him and advised him to be patient. Things were changing in baseball, and Rickey was going to be instrumental in effecting the change.

Roy left without knowing exactly what Rickey had in mind. But shortly afterward, he read that Jackie Robinson had been signed by Rickey to play for the Dodgers' Number 1 farm team at Montreal.

That was a real breakthrough. Roy figured that it would only be a matter of time before he got his chance.

In the meantime, he went to Venezuela to play winter ball. There he met Robinson for the first time. They talked about the new day that was dawning for the black player in baseball. In the early spring, about the time that Robinson returned to the States to report to his new ball club, Campy was summoned back to Brooklyn. Mr. Rickey, true to his word, signed Roy to a contract and shipped him to the Dodgers' minor-league affiliate at Nashua, New Hampshire.

"All I wanted was a chance in organized ball," said Campy. "I didn't care where they sent me."

He made the most of his chance. At Nashua, Roy proved to be a brilliant receiver. This surprised no one. But what did surprise everyone was the way he hit. His stance altered by Manager Walter Alston, Campy batted a crisp .290 and collected thirteen homers and ninety-six RBI's. He was promoted the following season to Montreal, where he led the International League's catchers in fielding percentage, putouts and assists. His batting average was .273.

In effect, Roy was doing what Robinson had not done—he was working his way up the line just like any other player, white or black. Still, Campy's good marks with Montreal earned him an opportunity to train with Brooklyn in the spring of 1948.

He played so well that he was carried on the roster till May. Then Rickey told him he was shipping him to St. Paul for a little more seasoning.

If Campy had been the type to sulk—and he wasn't—he wouldn't have had much time to nurse his pride. Determined to play his way up to the Dodgers, he caught and hit brilliantly for the Saints. Thus, a little more than a month later, when the Dodgers went into a tailspin, Manager Leo Durocher begged for Campy. Rickey responded by sending for him.

During his Dodger career, Campy's great years paralleled those of the team. And, of course, he contributed heavily to the Dodger success story. But in 1956, hampered by a severed nerve in his hand, he slumped to a .219 mark, though he still was healthy enough to catch 124 games and deliver twenty homers. His condition improved slightly in 1957; he hit .242 with thirteen homers.

But it was becoming clear that Campy was reaching the latter stages of his playing days. He now admitted to being thirty-six years of age, but there were some people who suspected he was older than that. Still, he was confident that he had a couple of good years left.

Then, on a cold, icy January night in the winter of 1958, as Roy drove home to his family in Glen Cove, Long Island, his car skidded into a pole and turned over. He remained barely conscious, pinned helplessly against the wheel. He was afraid the car

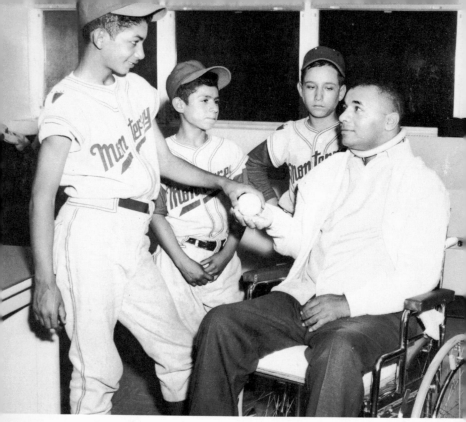

Since his accident, Campy has stayed close to the game. Here he greets Monterey, Mexico's Little League champions.

might catch on fire, but when he tried to reach out to turn off the ignition key, he discovered he couldn't move his arm. People in the neighborhood who had heard the car turn over came out to see what had happened. Soon an ambulance arrived and took Campanella away to a hospital. There, doctors operated on him to save his life. Fans everywhere prayed that he would live.

He did live, but he was hopelessly paralyzed. He

would never play ball again, probably never walk again. Roy underwent a rigid program of therapy to regain whatever muscular control he could. He was dogged in his efforts. His spirit was unquenchable. After a visit to his hospital room, Carl Erskine came out marveling, "He's the same old Campy. He's got the same round face and he's always smiling. Just talking to him there, I got the impression that he was more concerned about how bad the team was doing than about his own condition."

In the years since his accident, Roy has become a familiar figure at ballparks again, making appearances in a wheel chair at oldtimers' games. He has hosted his own radio and television shows, and counseled groups of boys on baseball and other aspects of life. Always, his good humor and bright outlook have shone through.

Baseball gave Campanella its ultimate honor in 1969. Along with fellow greats Stan Musial, Waite Hoyt and Stan Coveleskie, Campy was elected to baseball's Hall of Fame at Cooperstown.

It was there that Campanella, always a man to his ardent followers, gave his philosophy of the game he loved so much. "I have always believed," Campy said in his induction speech, "that any professional athlete, to be good, has to have a little bit of boy in him."

Mickey Cochrane

In the spring of 1925 Connie Mack, founder of one of baseball's earliest franchises, the old Philadelphia Athletics, had a young catcher named Gordon Cochrane. Cochrane was a black-haired, black-eyed Irish kid who played baseball with tremendous heart and spirit. He was cocky yet level-headed, and before the training season was over he had run the Athletics' regular catcher out of his job.

Later, when someone asked Mack what he had seen in Cochrane that led him to entrust the youth with such a vital job, the venerable old gentleman and former catcher replied: "The surprising thing about Cochrane is the quickness with which he learned to handle pitchers. During the first days of the season, I used to check his judgment by calling silently the types of pitches I thought he ought to choose. I'd say under my breath, 'now a fastball inside,' or 'now a slow curve,' or 'now a change of pace.' And I found that he was matching my judgment so much of the time that I discarded my original idea of giving him bench experience. I had, at the start, intended to sit him beside me and to coach him on pitching methods. He never really needed it."

Given the support and confidence of Mack, Cochrane embarked early on a career that was to establish him as one of the greatest catchers of all time. Indeed, even today, with baseball moving into the 1970s, many experts still insist he is the best. Certainly, in any debate, Cochrane's name invariably ranks among the first mentioned.

As a catcher, he was virtually without a flaw. As a leader, he was a firebrand who urged the best out of his pitchers. Some people contended that he did not possess a strong throwing arm, and they offered as testimony the 1931 World Series when the Cardinals' Pepper Martin stole five bases while Cochrane was catching. But those who rose to his defense reminded the critics that a baserunner steals against a pitcher far more often than he does on the catcher, because most pitchers do not know how to keep a runner properly close to the bag.

Cochrane came along at a time when baseball was still evolving as the national sport. He had begun his career as a catcher at the time Babe Ruth was establishing himself as the home-run hero who captured the imagination of the fans and shaped the image of the game forever. By his very talent and combativeness, Cochrane helped raise baseball to the status of a super sport.

But his beginnings were so modest that few could predict the great career that awaited him. He was a quiet, awkward-looking youngster when he was discovered on the athletic fields of Boston University, where he was majoring in business administration. He was good—though not spectacular—at sports and went out for the football team as a scrub. One day, just before the season opener, the Boston coach sent him in at halfback in a scrimmage against the varsity. On his first play, Cochrane took the ball and smashed into the line. Evading the grasps of the interior lineman, he barreled and feinted his way through the secondary. He didn't stop running until he had crossed the goal line.

This was the first indication that Cochrane might be an athlete of some prowess. He was promoted to the varsity and became one of the finest running backs in Boston University history. He also boxed and played on the baseball team. As an outfielder who swung a good bat, he seemed little different from hundreds of other young college baseball players of the period.

On spring days, Cochrane and his classmates liked to sit and sun themselves on the steps of the College of Business building. Directly across the street was the Hotel Brunswick, where visiting ball clubs stayed when they came to Boston to play the Braves or Red Sox. Cochrane would look enviously across at the ballplayers as they came and went. He wished he were one of them. "That is an ideal life," he would say. "Here today, New York tomorrow, Chicago next week. And a game of ball every day."

While still in college, Cochrane began playing summer baseball for the Dover, Delaware team in the Eastern Shore League. He was a good hitter and he preferred playing the outfield. One day the club's only catcher suffered a split finger and Jiggs Donohue, the Dover manager, looked at the rugged Cochrane and told him to go in and catch.

"I don't want to catch," Cochrane said.

"You'll catch, one way or another," Donohue said. "Either a baseball for me or a freight for Boston."

Cochrane got the message and donned the catching equipment for the first time in his life. He quickly mastered the basics and nobody ever thought of returning him to the outfield again. After batting .327 at Dover in 1923, Cochrane caught the eye of several major-league scouts and the bargaining for the big black-haired kid began in earnest. Tom Turner, a scout for Portland, won out over the others and signed Cochrane for the 1924 season. In the faster company of the Pacific Coast League he hit .333.

The following year, Connie Mack's Athletics bought the Portland franchise and many people said he did it just to get Cochrane. In any event, Cochrane was in the A's camp at Fort Myers, Florida in 1925. Here, of course, he came under the watchful gaze of Mack, who sat ramrod straight on the bench, wearing civilian clothes and holding his inevitable scorecard. Mack missed very little and he didn't fail to see Cochrane's potential. Still, he felt the young man would benefit by sitting at his side learning and watching. Then Ralph Perkins, the Athletics' regular catcher, was forced to miss a game and the old man sent Cochrane in. That marked the end of Cochrane's bench-warming.

Spring training was still in progress when Cochrane had his first run-in with an umpire. It was a rude awakening. The Athletics were playing the

Mickey Cochrane got his start with the old Philadelphia Athletics.

Braves, and the umpire behind home plate was Bill Klem, generally considered the best in the business. But whenever Klem called a ball when Cochrane thought he should have called a strike, the young catcher would hold onto the ball for a few extra seconds to indicate his displeasure.

Klem decided to put an instant halt to Cochrane's antics. Whipping off his mask, he glowered at the young receiver. "Young man," he said, "you are new in this game and I'm an old-timer, so I'm going to be patient. But if you want to stay in the major leagues, stop holding those balls. Get started right by realizing that the umpires in these leagues represent the last word of law and righteousness."

"Yes sir," said Cochrane and he pulled his mask back down over his reddened face.

The incident taught Cochrane never to try to intimidate umpires in front of the fans, but it did nothing to squelch his ready spirit. Despite his youth—he was now twenty-two—nobody called him "kid" any more. Because he was Irish, his teammates nicknamed him Mickey. It was as tough a name as they could think of. The name stuck—and so did Cochrane. He got into 134 games as a rookie and batted .331.

Despite his glowing year, critics were not convinced he was a major leaguer. He was still crude behind the plate and showed some defensive flaws. But he made up for these deficiences with his aggressive, take-charge nature. He never backed away from a challenge or another player. Judging him as a hitter, one opposing player scoffed, "Wait till the pitchers get to know him better. Then we'll see how really good he is."

When Cochrane's average dipped to .273 the following year, the chorus of "I-told-you-so's" grew louder. But Mack paid no attention. He never once wavered in his support of Cochrane, and he continued to keep him in the lineup. "We need the spark of his enthusiasm," he declared.

Mack's confidence was rewarded. Mickey came roaring back in 1927 to begin a succession of spectacular seasons with the Athletics. He batted .338 as the Athletics finished in second place. The following year, he hit .293. He had become such a superb all-around performer that the sportswriters voted him the Most Valuable Player in the American League in 1928. They voted him the honor as much for his catching as for his hitting, for by now Mickey had noticeably sharpened his defensive work. He knew the hitters better than any other catcher in the league and he made unerring calls. He pounced on bunts and fired quick throws to nail the runners. He handled low pitches in the dirt and high-twisting foul pops with sure judgment and surer hands. And always, he was the barking, fiery leader who kept everybody on the team—and in the ballpark—on his toes.

For the next three years—1929-30-31—the Athletics were pennant winners and twice won the world championship. Cochrane was instrumental in the overall success of the team, as he cracked out averages of .331, .357 and .349. Even with such powerhouses in the lineup as Al Simmons and Jimmy Foxx, Cochrane was the man who gave the A's their spark. In the 1929 Series, he batted .400; the A's defeated the Chicago Cubs in five games. In the 1930 Series against the Cardinals, he hit homers in the first two games, and when St. Louis pitcher Burleigh Grimes knocked him down with a pitch in the fifth game, Mickey got right up and smashed a single through the box. The A's won in six games.

The 1931 Series was Pepper Martin's Series. The scrappy Cardinal outfielder collected twelve hits for an average of .500, knocked in five runs and stole five bases. Cochrane could do nothing to stop him. The "Wild Horse of the Osage" took liberties against him such as no one else had ever dared to take. But Cochrane was woefully below par physically during the Series. He had been playing hard for six straight years, catching virtually every game and playing every one of them full tilt. Although he was worn out, he chose to ignore the fact. Even when Connie Mack tried to get him to take an occasional rest, Mickey wouldn't hear of it.

He had two more solid years with the Athletics, hitting .293 in 1932 and .322 in 1933. But by this time the Athletics were in trouble. The economic recession that had begun in 1929 had become "The

Great Depression." Like many other business organizations, the Athletics were in financial trouble and Connie Mack had been forced to sell three of his stars—Al Simmons, Mule Haas and Jimmie Dykes—following the 1932 season. Even so, his losses continued to mount.

During the winter baseball meetings of 1933, Frank Navin, president of the Detroit Tigers, approached Mack. He told him the Tigers were looking for a manager and had decided that Cochrane was the man they wanted. Mack was reluctant to part with the great catcher he had tutored from the very beginning, but he was in desperate straits. He needed money if he was to keep his ballclub in business. He finally consented to a trade in which he gave Cochrane to the Tigers in return for $100,-000 and a young catcher named John Pasek.

The Tigers had been foundering in fifth place for two seasons before Cochrane arrived. Suddenly, under his inspirational leadership, they began to show their claws. Guiding a Tiger lineup that included Charley Gehringer, Hank Greenberg, Goose Goslin, Pete Fox and Marv Owen for hitters and Schoolboy Rowe and Tommy Bridges for pitchers, Mickey led the team to its first pennant victory in a quarter of a century. Mickey also succeeded in setting a fine example himself. He hit .320 in 129 games and for the second time in his career was named the league's Most Valuable Player.

The St. Louis Cardinals, Cochrane's old nemesis

from his Athletic days, provided the World Series competition for the Tigers that fall. The Series was well played, going the full seven games, with the Cards winning out. Once again, Pepper Martin was there to plague Mickey with his devilish antics on the base paths, including two more steals. But by then the Detroit fans could forgive Cochrane anything. They contented themselves with the pennant he had brought them.

Mickey provided Detroit with its second consecutive pennant in 1935, steering the club home three lengths in front of the Yankees. He had his usual good year at the plate, batting .319, and sparking the Tigers with the kind of leadership that had always characterized his playing and managing. This time the Cubs were the Tigers' opponents in the Series, and this time the Tigers were not defeated. They won their first world championship.

In the sixth and clinching game, with the score tied, 3-3, Mickey singled in the bottom of the ninth with one man out. He hustled his way to second as Gehringer hit an infield grounder. With two men out, Goose Goslin came through with a single to right and Cochrane streaked around third and scored the winning run. When he reached home plate, the delirious Mickey jumped up and down

(Top) *Few catchers were better hitters than Mickey.*

(Bottom) *The Cardinals ran the bases wildly against the Tigers in the 1935 Series. But here Mickey blocks Ducky Medwick at the plate.*

several times before he was mobbed by the entire Tiger bench.

The Tiger clubhouse was sheer bedlam long after the victory. Somebody handed Cochrane a loudspeaker and he told those who were close enough to hear him, "This is the happiest day of my life. It was the most sensational Series I ever played in. My greatest thrill in baseball was scoring that winning run." Mickey couldn't have realized it then, but this was to be his last hurrah.

The following season he was plagued by injuries right from the start. First, he severely mashed his finger. Then he was hit on the foot by a foul tip. After that, he began having difficulty with his eyes and stomach. By June, Mickey was in such poor health he was hospitalized for rest and treatment. Then he took time off for a recuperative period on a ranch in Wyoming. When he finally returned to Detroit, he had to sit in the stands while his team played. He didn't get back into uniform until quite late in the season. The Tigers somehow still managed to finish in second place. Mickey, who played in only forty-four games that season, batted .270. Clearly, his health was declining.

The great career came to a crashing end early in 1937. On May 25, Mickey brought the Tigers into Yankee Stadium for a showdown series with the Yankees, with whom they were battling for first place. In the third inning, Mickey hit a home run off Bump Hadley. His next time at bat in the fifth was his last. On a three-and-one count, Hadley fired a pitch inside. The ball came directly at Cochrane's head and Mickey threw up his hands to protect himself. But the ball struck him in the left temple. He crumpled to the ground, unconscious. Several Tiger players rushed up to him and carried him from the field to the Tiger dressing room.

He was taken to St. Elizabeth's Hospital, where an examination revealed that Mickey had suffered a triple fracture of his skull. He was in critical condition. For four days, doctors weren't certain that he would live, and an anxious nation waited for every bulletin on his condition. Specialists were rushed in from other parts of the country to give as-

Cochrane's career came to a crashing halt when he was hit by a pitched ball in 1937. (N. Y. Daily News)

sistance. Finally, he was out of danger and the doctors said he would recover.

Cochrane was transferred to a hospital in Detroit, where he spent six more weeks. In July, he was able to return to the ballclub. But, at age thirty-four, his playing days were clearly behind him and his tenure as manager was soon to be terminated. An inspired Tiger team made a strong run for the flag but finished second. They seemed to have everything it took to win a pennant except, of course, the dynamic on-the-field leadership of Mickey Cochrane.

But what Mickey had done down on the playing field would not soon be forgotten. In thirteen seasons he had compiled a lifetime batting mark of .320 and he had won the Most Valuable Player award twice. He didn't set any special records for catchers—he merely set an example for peerless work behind the plate. In 1947 he was elected to the Hall of Fame. In 1969, both Athletic and Tiger fans named Cochrane to their all-time teams.

Cochrane used to keep a scrapbook. Once, looking back over his career, he told a friend, "I guess I must be something of a hero to myself. Sometimes, when I turn the pages of those clipping books, I feel as though I am reading about another person."

When Cochrane left baseball, there were those who said that they would never see his like again. They were probably right. One of those admirers, a father in Oklahoma who thought Mickey Cochrane was the greatest ballplayer he had ever seen, made sure he would never forget Mickey. When his son was born, he decided to name the child for his favorite ballplayer.

The boy's name? Mickey Mantle.

Bill Dickey

In the spring of 1928, Miller Huggins, the wasp-ish little man who managed the New York Yankees, stood among a group of sportswriters and watched a lanky young catcher warm up a pitcher. "We have bought a young man," he said, "who is destined to be one of the greatest catchers in the game. I'm not kidding you. I have a hunch about this boy."

Though Huggins had never played an inning in the major leagues, he had a keen eye for baseball talent. He managed such established baseball giants of the day as Babe Ruth, Lou Gehrig and Tony Lazzeri. But Bill Dickey, the young man who had caught his eye this spring day, was to become one of Huggins' proudest exhibits.

Fans and baseball officials often have argued about who was the greatest catcher in the game. No matter how heated the debate grew, Bill Dickey's name was always in the forefront. To many "experts"—in and out of baseball—Dickey was the best ever. He had no flaw as a catcher. He was smart, aggressive and alert, possessing virtually all of the attributes of a great athlete, except speed. "I guess I was always too slow to play anywhere else," Bill once said. "But I love it back of the bat. To be a good catcher, you've got to want to be a catcher."

Dickey never stopped working at his trade. Aside from his technical excellence, he made a thorough and intensive study of all opposing hitters, learning their mannerisms, detecting their weaknesses. He mentally catalogued every hitter he ever saw and he could remember each man's slightest vulnerability. Once, in 1943, while Dickey was serving as a Navy lieutenant during the war, he was approached by an Army corporal in a Washington hotel.

"Hi, Bill," the corporal said. "I don't know whether you remember me."

"Sure I remember you," Dickey said. "We used to pitch you high and inside. When we pitched you outside, it was boom!—the ballgame." Then he gave the soldier a puzzled look. "Say, what's your name?"

Dickey once explained his reason for becoming a catcher. "When I was a boy," he said, "everyone wanted to be a pitcher. Then a few years later, when Babe Ruth was breaking records, everyone wanted to be a slugger. The emphasis is still on hitting. Catching is a hard, disagreeable job. But it gives an opportunity to heavy men who are slow runners. Then, too, catchers are well paid. If I had my choice to make over again, I'd still be a catcher."

But in the spring of 1928, Bill was not quite polished enough to catch in the big leagues. The Yankees kept him at Little Rock, Arkansas, for most of the year, then brought him up to New York for the last few games. He had batted an even .300 for the minor-league Travelers, then connected for three hits in fifteen at-bats for the Yanks, who were about to clinch another pennant. In the World Series, Bill sat on the bench and watched the great Yankees achieve a four-game sweep of the St. Louis Cardinals.

The following spring, Dickey had to battle Benny Bengough and John Grabowski for the regular catching job. Dazzled by the way Ruth and Gehrig sent batting-practice pitches sailing over the distant fences, Dickey tried to emulate them. But all he could manage were some monumentally high pop flies. One day, Huggins drifted over to Bill and said, "Young man, choke up on the bat and stop unbuttoning your shirt on every pitch. That way you'll be around here longer."

The advice seemed to help. Bill won the first-string job in 1929 and had an outstanding year at the plate. He batted .324 in 130 games and he led the league's catchers in assists. He followed this up with a .339 mark in 1930. He hit better than .300 in each of his first six seasons with the Yankees.

Though he wasn't a power hitter like his roommate, Gehrig, Dickey had developed into a timely and consistent slugger. In fact, some opposing clubs considered Bill the most dangerous hitter in the entire Yankee batting order whenever there was a base runner in scoring position.

"If I were a pitcher," St. Louis Brown outfielder Mel Almada said, "there are two men I'd hate to see come up to the plate with men on bases. They are Joe Cronin of the Red Sox and Bill Dickey of the Yankees. They are more dangerous in the pinch than any other hitters in the league."

"The safest way to pitch to Dickey with men on base," said baseball clown Al Schacht, "is low and *behind* him."

When Dickey's average dropped to .279 in 1935, he decided to alter his batting style. "I made myself over as a hitter. I started to pull the ball more, so I could hit more home runs in Yankee Stadium." His batting average zoomed to .362 in 1936. At the same time, Dickey changed his catching technique. He moved closer to the plate. Being tall, he could not get under the batter as most catchers do. But he edged in closer than he had been playing. "The closer you are," he observed, "the less danger there is in being hit by foul tips."

Perhaps the best example of Dickey's coolness in the clutch occurred during the 1939 World Series against the Cincinnati Reds. In the opening game, the Yankees' Red Ruffing was locked in a pitching

Dickey wielded a potent bat. For seventeen major-league seasons, he compiled a .313 average.

duel with Cincinnati's Paul Derringer. In the bottom of the ninth inning, with the score tied, 1-1, Charley "King Kong" Keller tripled for the Yankees with one out. A deep fly ball, or almost any kind of hit, would bring in the winning run. The next Yankee batter was Joe DiMaggio, and the Reds decided to walk him intentionally. That brought up Dickey. Bill had been hitless all day so the Reds figured he would be easier to pitch to than DiMaggio. Cincinnati Manager Bill McKechnie was hopeful that Derringer could coax the slow-running Dickey to hit a ground ball for a double play to end the inning. But Dickey came through with a ringing liner to centerfield and Keller trotted home with the winning run.

The Yanks took the first three games of the Series. In the fourth game, Derringer again was the opposing pitcher. Early in the game, the powerful Keller homered to give New York a 1-0 lead. Mc-Kechnie felt that as long as Derringer was on the mound, the Reds could stay close. But in the seventh inning, Dickey came up and smashed a homer into the stands in right-center. This changed Mc-Kechnie's strategy, and he was forced to take Derringer out of the game for a pinch-hitter. The Reds managed to rally and tie the score, but with Derringer out the Yankees eventually won, 7-4, in extra innings to capture yet another World Series.

In the Reds' locker room after the game, Derringer asked a sportswriter, "Who do you think is the best player on the Yankees?"

"Joe DiMaggio," the writer said bluntly.

"Nope, not for my money," said Derringer. "I'll take Dickey before DiMaggio from what I've seen of him in this Series, and I don't say that because he singled to beat me in the first game and then hit that homer off me today."

"Why, then?" the writer asked.

"Because of the way he handles pitchers and because of the way he leads the team," Derringer said. "He's something more than a great hitter. He's a great thinker, and mechanically, he's just about a perfect catcher."

Seated a few feet away, Cincinnati third-baseman Billy Werber agreed with Derringer. "You can give Dickey a lot of credit for the great pitching of the Yankees," he said. "Take a flighty fellow like Monte Pearson. He pitches a two-hit game against us only because Dickey's there to steady him down when he starts getting wild. Dickey watches the batter's feet as he stands up at the plate and from that can tell what the batter is looking for. He's really smart."

Dickey's judgment was rarely challenged by Yankee pitchers. He knew precisely what pitch to call for in a given situation, and the pitchers had the utmost confidence in his calls. Managers, too, had total reliance in him. Before the start of one World Series game, Manager Joe McCarthy held a pre-game strategy session with his players. As the meeting was about to break up, he turned to Dickey and to left-handed pitcher Marius Russo, who was to start the game that day, and said, "All right, you two fellows can have the next half-hour to get your plans together."

Dickey went off to a corner of the room with Russo, where the pitcher said, "Look, let's have it this way, Bill. You just give me the signal and I'll throw to your glove." That was it, period. The conversation lasted ten seconds. Russo went out and pitched a four-hitter.

On the infrequent occasions when pitchers disagreed with him, Dickey never seemed to mind. "When they shake me off," he explained, "I let them throw what they want to. I don't argue with a pitcher. He's the fellow who's got to throw the ball and it's always better to let him use the curve or fastball in which he has the most confidence."

Perhaps the greatest tribute to Dickey's ability to call pitches came from Bob Feller of the Cleveland Indians during his peak years. "If I had Dickey catching me," he said, "I believe I could win thirty-five games a year."

With all of the greatness attached to his career, Dickey never truly got all of the credit he deserved. There were the inescapable comparisons to Mickey Cochrane, who was fiery and combative. Dickey was neither colorful nor dramatic. He was a quiet man, whose nature matched very nearly that of his roommate, Lou Gehrig. Neither ever had very much to say, and Dickey expressed himself best by what he did on the playing field.

He spent sixteen seasons in the big leagues, all of them with the Yankees. Though he never won a batting title or a league award, he did compile an enviable lifetime batting average of .313. He set records for batting in five runs in a single World Series game and belting homers with the bases loaded in two consecutive games. Not even Babe Ruth ever did that. Of the catching records he established, most have since been broken; but the feats remain remarkable just the same. Six times he led the American League in fielding. In 1931, he posted the highest fielding average for a catcher in one season—.996. And he once went through

Bill fearlessly charges into the stands for a foul ball.

125 games without being charged with a passed ball. He was the American League's All-Star catcher eleven out of a possible twelve times. But the true test of Dickey's durability is his record of catching 100 or more games a season for thirteen consecutive years.

"I tried to copy Cochrane," Dickey admitted late in his career. "But I was so much taller that I couldn't get my right leg back the way he did. When I made myself over in 1936, I started using a lighter, smaller glove. I learned the trick of catching many pitches with one hand. This saved my right hand from foul tips." Not until his playing days were nearly over did Bill reveal that his thumb and every finger on his throwing hand had been broken by foul tips.

Before the start of the 1944 season, Bill entered the United States Navy. Upon his discharge in early 1946, he was thirty-nine years old. Most observers felt his playing career was at an end. But Bill spoke optimistically of making a comeback. In his last pre-war year, he had batted .351 in eighty-five games. But when spring training rolled around, he was clearly not his old self. His timing was off and he was slower-footed than ever. Only his arm retained a spark of greatness. Bill relived some of his past one day in May when he cut down two runners on the base paths.

But the event that nudged him into retirement was not his aging body and reflexes. Joe McCarthy became ill and, on doctor's orders, resigned as Yankee manager. One hour after McCarthy notified the club, the Yanks announced that Dickey would be their new manager. But the job was too much for Bill to handle. He now was expected to command a team of players with whom he had been friends for many years. The adjustment was an almost impossible one for him to make. In September, with the Yankees on a losing streak and falling to third place, Bill made a decision which he felt was in the best interest of a team he had served so well for sixteen years. He asked that he not be considered for the manager's job in 1947, and his resignation was accepted on the spot.

Two years later, however, Dickey ended his brief retirement from baseball. Casey Stengel had become the manager, and he hired Bill to teach a young man named Larry Berra the benefits of his long years of experience as a catcher. Dickey was happy again. He was one of the few who had faith in Berra's ability to develop into a respectable catcher. After coaching Berra for a week, Dickey reported, "He has the makings of a good catcher. I can't say a great one, but I wouldn't be surprised if he is even that some day. Right now, he does just about everything wrong, but I was warned about that. He can move, and that's the main idea."

William Malcolm Dickey was born in Bastrop, Louisiana, on June 6, 1907. He had two sisters and two brothers. One younger brother, George, was also a big-league catcher for several years. Bill's father was a railroad man, who moved the family often throughout the South. By the time Bill was in his teens, the family was settled in Little Rock. Bill attended Little Rock College, where he was a pitcher and a catcher on the baseball team.

"I wasn't much of a pitcher," Bill said. "I remember that I used to alternate—three innings of catching and then three innings of pitching." But when Bill was only eighteen and still in high school, he got a job catching for a semipro nine in Hot Springs, not very far from his home. There he was spotted by Bob Allen, owner of the Little Rock minor-league team of the Southern Association. Dickey went to play for Little Rock in 1925, getting into

When his days were over, Dickey taught his protégé, Yogi Berra, the art of catching.

only three games. Manager Lena Blackburne saw in him the potentials of a top catcher, but Bill still had a lot of flaws in his game then.

"He was a pretty crude catcher when I first saw him," Blackburne recalled. "I remember the day I saw him play for the Hot Springs team. I went there to look over a third-baseman, but signed Dickey instead even though he threw a ball against the rightfield fence trying to pick a man off first. I could see that he had a strong arm."

After failing to stick with Little Rock, Bill went to Muskogee, Oklahoma, in the Western Association in 1926. There, his professional training got off the ground. Bill was behind the plate virtually every day, learning the intricacies of the job, picking up tips from other catchers and constantly making mental notes. His baseball education was interrupted briefly when the Muskogee team met with financial failure. Dickey divided his time among Little Rock, Jackson, Mississippi, and Buffalo for the next year and a half, before the Yankees finally bought his contract for $15,000.

"Gosh, I sure was scared," Bill reminisced about the purchase. "I didn't think I was worth so much money. And then to be on the same team with Babe Ruth, Tony Lazzeri, Lou Gehrig, Joe Dugan, Herb Pennock and Earle Combs sure was enough to frighten a green kid. But they were good fellows and they made it easy for me to break in."

Throughout his career, Dickey was known as an

Dickey was part of the Murderers' Row batting order of the Yankees, along with Joe DiMaggio, right.

affable person, and a man who rarely lost his composure. But on one particular day Bill's even temper was challenged severely. In the Yankee clubhouse, Red Ruffing decided to needle Bill about his lack of running speed. Pretending not to see Dickey, who was sitting nearby, Ruffing said to coach Art Fletcher: "You know, the Babe Ruth is slowing down in the outfield. How about teaching him to throw right-handed and making a catcher out of him? Then he wouldn't have to run."

Fletcher, sizing up the situation, replied, "That's not a bad idea." Then he turned to Dickey and said innocently, "What do you think, Bill?"

Dickey, no longer able to hold himself back, glared at the two men. "Why not make a pitcher out of him?" Bill said caustically. "Then he wouldn't even have to think."

Bill Dickey could make such a remark. He had done the thinking for a lot of championship pitchers.

Bill Freehan

Surrounded by his important callers from the Detroit Tigers, nineteen-year-old Bill Freehan felt his head spinning. The three men—General Manager Jim Campbell, Vice President Rick Ferrell and scout Lou D'Annunzio—had come to his home the moment he was eligible to sign a professional contract, and now they sat around fidgeting while Bill and his dad considered their offer.

He would come high—everyone knew that. Bill was a sophomore at the University of Michigan, but already his hitting and catching had attracted scouts from every major-league team. All had sent back glowing reports. But Bill was a Detroit boy, born and raised there, and this made the Tigers feel they had the inside track on him.

Still, they sat nervously when the phone rang and Ashley Freehan, Bill's dad, listened to a rival offer from the Kansas City Athletics. Finally, they heard him say, "Thank you very much, Mr. Finley, but we're going to stick with the Tigers."

The three visitors breathed a collective sigh of

relief, and in short order had Bill's signature on a contract of rare generosity. The Tigers were agreeing to a contract of $175,000 for the privilege of making him into a major-league catcher. The money was enough to send the eyes of any normal nineteen-year-old spinning around in his head. Bill's eyes spun. He was young, talented—and instantly rich. In a little more than two years, he would be playing in the majors. Oh, how Mickey Cochrane and Bill Dickey would have loved to be raised in the time of Bill Freehan!

Admittedly, it didn't come easy for Bill, and certainly, he didn't come into the majors fully equipped. But along with his raw ability and a rock-hard body that measured 6 feet 3 inches and 195 pounds, he had a certain mental toughness and maturity to accept any challenge.

The Tigers sent Bill to Duluth-Superior in the Northern League for the 1961 season. He arrived with a high opinion of himself, gathered during his sandlot and college days. Some of the older professionals resented his immediate take-charge attitude. But it was Bill's fixed notion that the catcher ran a ballgame, whether he was nineteen years old or thirty-nine years old. As left-handed pitcher Mickey Lolich, one of his teammates at Duluth-Superior remembered, "He was brand new, and he sort of tried to take over, to let everyone know how much he knew. He wanted you to do everything his way, and I didn't like that."

Whether his teammates liked it or not, Bill refused to change. But he backed up his brashness with his performance on the field. He batted .343 with seven homers and twenty-six runs-batted-in in his first thirty games, and the Tigers decided to promote him to Knoxville, which was quite a jump for a kid with his limited experience. Only two months earlier, he had still been in college. At Knoxville, Bill hit .289, the first time in his life that he batted below .300. Still, at the tail end of the season, the Tigers gave him another change of uniform. He was summoned to Detroit and given a Tiger uniform.

His first glimpse of the big leagues didn't seem to faze the strapping young catcher. It was late September and the Tigers wanted to take a good look at their expensive new acquisition. They couldn't have picked a better game for Bill to make

Freehan, in the batting cage, practices his powerful swing.

his debut. In a game filled with base hits and walks and steals, Bill had the thrill of throwing out his first major-league baserunner. He had the thrill of getting his first major-league hits, too, as he singled in his first two trips to the plate. He wound up his brief trial with the Tigers with an average of .400.

That first flush of success didn't exactly mean Bill was ready to stick in the majors. There was still plenty of schooling ahead and he grudgingly acknowledged it. He went to Denver in 1962 and spent the entire season there. He appeared in 113 games, batted .283 with nine homers and fifty-eight RBI's, and he was the top fielding catcher in the American Association with a percentage of .985. Back in the Detroit front office, there was a growing belief that he might be ready now.

In the spring of 1963, Freehan went to the Tigers' instructional school to improve his catching. The school was run by Charlie Dressen, a veteran major-league manager. Dressen came from the old school. He believed ballplayers shouldn't be coddled and had to earn their place in the big leagues. He had an alert baseball brain, but he wasn't exactly bowled over by cocky young, college-bred kids with big bonuses. He singled Bill out for special hazing, and at first, Bill was taken aback by it. When Bill allowed a runner coming home from third to knock the ball out of his glove, Dressen teased him about the softness of college life. Bill bristled, but kept his mouth shut. He was sensible enough to realize he was learning something under the cagey Dressen.

The betting was heavy that Bill wouldn't stick with the Tigers in 1963, but somehow he survived the cuts and went to Detroit for the opening of the season. Gus Triandos was the team's regular catcher. One day, Manager Bob Scheffing decided to use Bill. Scheffing found he couldn't get Bill out of the lineup. The rookie catcher responded by getting on base nine consecutive times, collecting three homers, three doubles, a triple and two singles in fifteen times at bat.

Three months into the season, the Tigers replaced Scheffing with Bill's old nemesis, Charlie Dressen. But instead of sending him to the sidelines, Dressen allowed Bill to share the catching duties with the veteran Triandos. That didn't mean he got off his back. "He was always on the kid," said a seasoned Tiger player. "He'd really give it to Bill in the meetings. Bill would try to talk back a little, but he was no match for Dressen. Most of the time he would just sit there and take it."

Freehan took the guff because he was intelligent enough to realize that Dressen had a method to his madness. "I used to say to myself, what's he always picking on me for—I'm the youngest guy out there," Bill said. "I was doing the best I could. But then I began thinking about it. I finally realized that this was the man's way of trying to teach me something. It got so that I didn't mind it at all. In

Freehan slides under rival catcher John Roseboro of the Minnesota Twins to score a run for the Tigers.

fact, I began to feel that the more he kept after me, the better it made me play."

Bill wound up an impressive rookie year. He batted .243 with nine homers and thirty-six RBI's in 100 games, and his defensive skills were beginning to be appreciated. Even Dressen said, "At the rate he's going, he'll be the Number One catcher in baseball before he's twenty-five. With a player like him, the Tigers should have no catching problems for years to come."

The Tigers were so convinced that Dressen was right that they traded Triandos away in the off-season, virtually handing the first-string job to Freehan. With all his confidence, Bill still knew his limitations. The Tiger pitching staff he was catching was essentially a veteran one. They knew more baseball than he did and he knew they didn't like having their game caught for them by a youngster. In a clubhouse meeting, Freehan once told them, "Look, you guys have been pitching a long time. Just throw your game, and I'll try to catch up. If you don't like the signals I put down, that's okay."

Still, Dressen wanted him to become more aggressive. Bill gradually began to assert himself. Despite his youth, he had the command and the presence of a leader, and amazingly, the Tigers seemed to respond to him. This became easier after Dressen began bringing in a corps of youthful hurlers, youngsters like Freehan himself, and the chemistry between pitcher and catcher became better.

With his own growing assurance and the confidence Dressen now showed in him, Bill had a splashy year in 1964. He batted an even .300 to become the first Detroit catcher since Mickey Cochrane to reach that figure. He also belted eighteen homers, drove in eighty runs and became the youngest catcher ever to be named to the All-Star squad. Technically, Freehan was becoming a good catcher. While he didn't possess a great arm, he was learning to get his throws away quickly. Still to be sharpened was his skill in calling a game. When the Tigers had mostly veteran pitchers, Bill deferred to them. Now, with younger pitchers, he still seemed a little hesitant in taking charge, and this resulted in their not being quite sure of him. Having doubts in their catcher can cause unrest in pitchers, and Dressen kept trying to inspire Bill to be more forceful in his handling of the staff.

But a conflict developed after Dressen's death in 1966. The Tigers underwent a period of interim managers. Bob Swift, who replaced Dressen, also died, and Frank Skaff ran the club for the remainder of the season. But in 1967, Mayo Smith became the new manager. He hired Johnny Sain as pitching coach. Sain was a former pitcher and he believed that pitchers, not catchers, should be in charge of their own ballgames. So, the young aces of the Detroit staff would often be seen shaking off Bill's signs and he would have to go to the mound to talk to them. Ultimately, Bill straightened things out with each of his pitchers.

He also straightened out a hitting problem in 1967. In his two previous seasons, he had slumped at the plate, batting .234 each year. Part of the problem was attributed to a back ailment which had plagued him off and on. Another reason was a hitting flaw that finally was detected in 1967 when Mayo Smith hired Wally Moses as the Tigers' batting coach. Moses, a former American League batting star, immediately saw that Bill wasn't hitting through the ball properly. He worked with Bill daily and got him to move closer to the plate.

Improvement was immediately visible, as Bill had a standout year in 1967. He batted .282 with

Bill prepares to tag out the Twins' Zoilo Versalles.

twenty homers and seventy-four runs-batted-in. He caught more games than any other catcher in the majors, led American League receivers in putouts for the third consecutive year and caught all fifteen innings of the All-Star Game.

More important, he led the Tigers to one of their best campaigns in years. They were pennant contenders following the All-Star break, and Bill was the team's most dependable hitter in the clutch. At the end of the season, he was a strong candidate for Most Valuable Player. He may have won the award had the Tigers captured the flag. But they lost out on the final day of the season. Still, Freehan's performance during the long pennant race prompted rival Manager Ed Stanky of the Chicago

White Sox to say, "Detroit's MVP is the catcher. He might be the whole league's. The Tigers lose Freehan, and they're out of it."

The Tiger catching star was born in Detroit on November 29, 1941, the eldest of four Freehan children. He grew up in a city neighborhood which he liked to refer to as being tough. But in reality, he had a comfortable middle-class upbringing. "All my energy was expended in sports," he has said, recalling a boyhood where baseball, football and basketball dominated his days. He was always big for his age, so he wound up playing with boys older than himself. Bill was a shortstop until his Little League team's catcher failed to show up one day and he was put behind the plate. The only serious trouble he ever got into occurred when he and some friends engaged in a contest tossing rotten tomatoes onto a neighbor's roof. A policeman, who also happened to be Bill's Little League coach, came by and reprimanded them. "If you have to throw something," he told them, "throw a baseball."

In 1955, when Bill was fourteen, the family moved to St. Petersburg, Florida, where Ashley Freehan had bought a mobile-home camp. Bill entered Bishop Barry High and joined all the athletic teams. Baseball and football were his best sports. During the summers, he returned to Detroit and played sandlot ball. It was during one of these summers that he first caught the eye of Lou D'An-

At the University of Michigan, Freehan was a star in both football and baseball as a sophomore.

nunzio. Bill was 6 feet 2 inches tall and 185 pounds, and D'Annunzio immediately tabbed him as the best sandlot catcher he had ever seen.

At D'Annunzio's suggestion, general manager Jim Campbell came around to see Bill play. Campbell vividly remembers his first impression of Freehan. "The moment I saw all the players on the field, I picked him out at once," he said. "I never saw such coordination in a big athlete."

The colleges, too, were interested in Bill, and he began sifting through a flock of offers. He rejected a scholarship from Notre Dame because he was told he would not be permitted to play both football and baseball. He accepted one from the University of Michigan, which imposed no restrictions. In two years at Ann Arbor, Bill became a spectacular athlete, starring at end on the football team and as a hitting catcher with the baseball squad. In his sophomore year, he batted over .500 to set a Big Ten record, and now the big-league scouts renewed their pressure to get him to sign a professional contract. Such big-name people as Ted Williams, representing the Boston Red Sox, and Ralph Houk, manager of the Yankees, hawked the Michigan campus and visited his home. The Orioles were practically ready to pawn their franchise for him. And the Tigers wined and dined the Freehans on several occasions.

All of this pressure simply was too much for him, and Bill and his dad finally made the decision to go with the Tigers. Bill's ultimate reason for picking

Bill, like teammate Al Kaline, right, was an instant hero in Detroit.

Detroit was based on money, the opportunity for quick advancement plus his lifelong interest in the team. When Bill was eligible to sign a professional contract at the termination of the 1961 college baseball season, Jim Campbell, Rick Ferrell and Lou D'Annunzio made their trek over to the Freehan house.

As Bill went into his fifth major-league season, established as the best catcher in the American League, there was no doubt either about who the team leader was. The Tigers jumped out to a big lead and looked as if nobody would head them off in their drive for their first pennant since 1945. The pitching staff, led by Denny McLain, who went on to win thirty-one games, was superb. The hitting all season of Freehan, Al Kaline, Willie Horton and Norm Cash, sent the runs flying across the plate. Detroit clinched the flag on September 17, with relatively few problems along the way. But on the few occasions the Tigers ran into trouble, it was Freehan who lifted their sagging spirits, either with a key base hit or with a well-chosen word of encouragement in the locker room.

Mickey Lolich, who had once complained back in the low minors when Bill tried to take over too quickly, now said, "It's so different now. I like working with him. We work well together."

And Bill Freehan, who walked tall among all the Tigers, merely shrugged and said, "I worked all my life to be better than the other guy."

Gabby Hartnett

In the baseball museum at Cooperstown, New York, there is a bronze plaque enshrining Gabby Hartnett in the Hall of Fame. Like all the other plaques at Cooperstown, Hartnett's is a lasting memorial to the playing career of one of baseball's all-time greats.

But there is another memento from Hartnett's playing days that is engraved just as deeply in the memories of thousands of baseball fans. It is a photo that shows Hartnett rounding third base in the growing darkness at Wrigley Field in September, 1938, with what looks like half the population of Chicago chasing him in happy pursuit.

The homer was the climactic blow of the 1938 National League pennant race, during which Hartnett, the catcher-manager of the Cubs, rallied his team to overtake the Pittsburgh Pirates on the next-to-the-last day of the season. At one point late in the season, the Cubs had been seven games behind. From the look on Hartnett's face in the photo, one would deduce he was the most popular man in

Chicago that day. The truth is he probably was. But he had achieved such a status only after a long and successful stay with the Cubs. It was a far cry from the way he had been received the first time he came to Chicago sixteen years earlier.

Hartnett was a shy youngster of twenty-one who had never been very far from his home in Millville, Massachusetts, until the Cubs signed him for the 1922 season. He arrived in Chicago, where he would spend three days before going on to the Pacific Coast to begin spring training with the Cubs. "For three long days I walked around that big city," he recalled years later. "I knew not a soul. I had no friends. I took in all the sights, spent many hours in my hotel, saw a few shows and did anything to amuse myself and kill time. Throughout the three days, I did not speak to a single person. At the end of the third day, I found an alley where I knew I was out of hearing distance and let out a great big 'Hello!' I wanted to be sure I still had my voice."

The following day, he was on a westbound train for the Coast. On the same train were a few other ballplayers and some newspapermen. Hartnett didn't know anyone else, so he kept to himself and spoke to no one. Finally, a Chicago sportswriter named Eddie Sullivan seated himself next to the reserved young man, saying, "You sure are a *gabby* guy, aren't you? Why don't you ever say something?"

That is precisely how Leo Hartnett got his nick-name of "Gabby."

"I was afraid I'd pull a boner," he admitted. "I didn't want to appear to be a fresh kid."

The 1922 Cubs trained on Catalina Island off the California coast. Hartnett, who was the rawest of rookies with only one previous year of profes-sional experience, didn't get much of a chance to show what he could do. But he was befriended by the great Grover Cleveland Alexander, one of the game's foremost pitchers. Alexander was an old acquaintance of Hartnett's father and he took a lik-ing to the boy. The relationship was fortunate for Hartnett.

Hartnett had another friend, too, in scout Jack Doyle, who signed him. When the Cubs returned to the mainland to open an exhibition series in Los Angeles, they held a meeting to discuss trimming the roster of excess players. "I'm going to send Hartnett out for farming," said Manager Bill Kille-fer.

"But he hasn't caught a game yet," protested Doyle. "Why not give him that chance first?"

Killefer reluctantly agreed. Hartnett was in the contingent of players that went to Cincinnati for the season's opener. When Alexander was sched-uled to pitch the first game, he insisted that Hart-nett be his catcher. Normally, a pitcher would have very little say about who his catcher should be, but Alexander enjoyed a special status. Killefer decided to let him have his way. It was only for one game, after all. Once his trial was over, Hartnett could be shipped off to the minors.

The Cincinnati fans who turned out for the opener thus saw an unusual starting battery for the Cubs—a grizzled veteran with 250 pitching victories in eleven years, and a rawboned youngster who actually was witnessing, as well as catching, his first major-league game. If Gabby was nervous, he didn't really show it. Once or twice he bobbled a pitch, and Alexander came down off the mound to settle him. "Take care, kid," he said. "I'll pitch 'em and you hold 'em, okay?" Gabby nodded and went back behind the plate.

"You can imagine how I felt then," he recalled some years later. "Here we were, starting the season—I, a rookie behind the bat, and the great Alexander out there in the pitcher's box. True, Alex and I had become pals to a certain extent off the field. But I was all nervousness when it came right down to the pinch. To him, it was an old story."

Still, the veteran and the rookie came through with flying colors for the Cubs. Alex coasted to a 7-3 win and Hartnett, the quiet kid behind the mask, singled once in his four times at bat. His own fears calmed by Alexander's patient handling, Gabby appeared poised behind the plate. In truth, Alex probably did more to get his catcher through the game than Hartnett did to help his pitcher.

"My successful debut was as much due to Alex-

Hartnett set home run records with his big swing.

ander's encouragement as to any ability that I may have had," Hartnett said in later years.

Following the game, Alexander went up to the still skeptical Killefer, who had been a top catcher himself in his playing days, and said, "The kid's all right, Bill. Stick with him."

"I've had a good many nice things written about me and said about me," Hartnett said. "But that little speech of old Alex is the one I remember.

I've still got the ball that was in play when that game ended, and I treasure it, as I do the glove I used. Alex fanned Babe Pinelli for the last out. That's how I happened to get the ball."

A couple of days later, in a game against the Cardinals, Killefer sent Gabby up to pinch-hit for pitcher Vic Aldridge with two Cub runners on base. A left-hander named Bill Bailey was on the mound for St. Louis. Gabby picked out a fastball and drilled it up the alley in right-center field. The hit sent both runners home and looked like an easy triple. But Hartnett, never taking his eyes off the ball, tripped over first base and fell to the ground. Hurriedly, he scrambled to his feet and raced for second, barely beating the relay throw from the outfield. The usually poker-faced Killefer had all he could do to keep from breaking out laughing.

Hartnett was never again in jeopardy of returning to the minors. Killefer kept him for the remainder of the 1922 season, and every time Alexander went out to pitch, Gabby was his catcher. As a result, he got into thirty-one games that year. Although he hit a meager .194, the Cubs could see that he had the makings of a hitter. With just two years of professional baseball behind him, he simply needed time to learn the pitchers.

Despite the fact that he made the club in 1923, Gabby again was assigned a seat on the bench, seemingly for a long stay. But when regular catcher Bob O'Farrell was hurt late in the season, Killefer rushed Gabby into the mask and pads. By the time O'Farrell was ready to return, he found that he had lost his job to the kid from Millville. Given his big chance, Gabby grew up overnight as a big-league receiver.

To Hartnett's great credit, he was a quick and willing student, always looking to pick up tips from other catchers. He was bright and ambitious. Though he had been timid and reserved when he first joined the club, he began to assert himself more, to take charge of the pitchers. He studied the hitters and learned their weaknesses. At the same time, he discovered what his own pitchers could do in given situations, and he learned to call for the right pitches.

For the next fourteen years, the Cubs never even thought of looking for another catcher. Gabby became widely acclaimed as the best in the league. He was strong and durable enough to establish a National League record by catching 100 or more games for twelve years, eight of them in a row. Physically, he was a hulking brute, standing 6 feet 1 inch tall and weighing 218 pounds. He was a tough and aggressive leader who could not be intimidated by hard-sliding baserunners. Oddly enough, Gabby had surprisingly small hands for a man his size—especially small hands for a catcher. But he had great strength in them. He could grip a ball firmly and wing it with power and accuracy to any base.

Charley Grimm, his manager in later years, paid him the supreme compliment. "Let's assume," he said, "that he's the greatest catcher you or I will ever see."

Hartnett won just as much praise for his hitting as for his defensive brilliance. It is one of the ironies of being a catcher that critics make note of one's defensive skills sooner if the catcher is also a good hitter. So, to Hartnett's benefit, he could hit. After batting a modest .268 in eighty-five games in 1923, he then catapulted into the top rank of the game's hitters with a .299 mark the following year. He batted .300 or better six times in his twenty big-league seasons and wound up with a lifetime average of .297.

Though he never led the league in home runs, he did manage to collect a career total of 236 and to hit as many as thirty-seven in one season. In fact once, early in the 1924 campaign, Gabby socked ten homers within a ten-day period, and fans thought they were witnessing the emergence of a new home-run star. He tailed off after that, hitting only six more the rest of the season.

For the next decade, Hartnett dominated the league's catchers—except for 1929, when he got into only twenty-five games due to the recurrence of an old childhood injury. As a result, he was reduced to three futile pinch-hitting appearances in the 1929 World Series, in which the Cubs faced Connie Mack's Philadelphia Athletics. The

Cubs were National League champions again in 1932, and this time they were opposed by the powerful New York Yankees. Though the Cubs were defeated in a four-game Series, Gabby distinguished himself by hitting .313 and establishing a Series record for catchers by chalking up five assists.

In 1933, a sportswriter named Arch Ward dreamed up the idea of staging a baseball all-star game in conjunction with the World's Fair scheduled for Chicago that year. This was the actual beginning of *the* All-Star Game, a one-season idea that became an annual event. Appropriately, Hartnett was selected as the National League's catcher.

This was to be one of five annual All-Star Games that he would catch. But the game with which he is most associated was played in 1934. Over a two-inning stretch, Carl Hubbell of the New York Giants struck out in order Babe Ruth, Lou Gehrig, Jimmy Foxx, Al Simmons and Joe Cronin, who represented the power and the pride of the American League. His performance remains as one of the great pitching feats of all time, and Hartnett was Hubbell's catcher that day.

But through his long years with the Cubs, Hartnett caught a procession of top pitchers, including Burleigh Grimes, Lon Warneke, Charley Root, Bill Lee, Claude Passeau and Dizzy Dean. Of them all, he rated Dean as the greatest. "I might straddle the issue and call Hubbell the greatest left-hander

Gabby caught some of the best pitchers in baseball history. The very best were Grover Alexander, left, and Dizzy Dean, right.

and old Diz the greatest right-hander," he said, "but I'll still take old Diz. Alexander, of course, was on the downgrade when I caught him."

Actually, Hartnett was instrumental in the Cubs' acquisition of Dean from the Cardinals. Dean had come down with a serious arm injury. But Hartnett was convinced that Diz could still pitch and he urged his bosses to go after him—at any cost. They did, handing over $185,000 and three players to obtain Dean in 1938. Dizzy may have lost his fabled fastball by then, but he had lost none of his guile or his competitiveness. With Hartnett guiding him, he won some big games for the Cubs and posted a 7-1 record. In one memorable game against the Giants, Dizzy allowed five hits and made only eighty-eight pitches, so perfect was his control that day.

"If I had that guy to pitch to all the time," Dean said of Hartnett, "I'd never lose me a game."

But Charley Root, who had joined the Cubs in 1923 and spent sixteen years as Hartnett's battery mate, summed it up best when he said, "He gets it out of you. If you're letting down, or inclined to get grumpy like Pat Malone used to do, Gabby will fire that ball back at you like a shot. Believe me, that wakes you up. My own experience with him catching is that he always calls for the right pitch. Many times, I've stood out there and figured that the thing to do was come in with a curve. I'd look for the signal, and that's what Gabby wanted. He was forever on the alert, and I think he has broken up more steals and more hit-and-run plays by calling for pitch-outs than any other catcher in baseball. He is daring at all times, and sure of himself. He makes a pitcher feel that way, too."

To no one's surprise, the Cubs chose Hartnett as their manager to replace Charley Grimm in 1938. Actually, Gabby had filled in as interim manager in 1937 when Grimm was hospitalized. "Hartnett was entitled to the job," said P. K. Wrigley, the Cubs' owner, "and he was Grimm's logical successor. But he was not made manager just for those reasons. I wanted to be sure first that he was the best man for the job. I studied the situation myself. I questioned hundreds of persons—fans, players, other managers, league executives, club owners and officials. Even umpires. Their opinion was unanimously for Hartnett."

Under player-manager Hartnett, the Cubs made a late-season run at the slumping Pirates, reeling off eight wins in a row. This still left them a half-game out of first place when they faced the Pirates on the next-to-the-last day of the season. As they went into the last half of the ninth inning, the score was tied, 5-5. There were two out for the Cubs and no one on base. With darkness rapidly enveloping the field, it was clear the game would be called after one more out. Up stepped Hartnett. He picked out one of Mace Brown's fastballs and rode it into the left-field stands for the game-winning homer that planted the Cubs in first place. The hero's welcome that he got after circling the bases made the next day's clinching win an anticlimax.

The National League was less than twenty-five years old and the twentieth century was in its first year when Charles Leo Hartnett was born on December 20, 1900. He was the first of nine children born to Mr. and Mrs. Fred Hartnett of Woonsocket, Rhode Island. Though he was to be known universally as Gabby when he became a professional ballplayer, his mother always called him Leo.

When Leo was about seven years old, the family

moved a few miles across the Massachusetts border to the tiny town of Millville. The town was just what its name suggests—a mill town—and almost everybody living there worked in the mill, including Fred Hartnett. Leo attended Longfellow Grammar, where he developed his first affection for baseball. One of his first games almost proved to be his last.

He was playing in the outfield one day when the hitter drove a ball far over his head. Leo chased after it at full speed. Simultaneously, another boy ran for the ball. In one of those senseless, unthinking moments boys seem to have, he gave Leo a playful shove which sent him tumbling to the ground. Leo was knocked unconscious by the fall and his right arm was splintered in several places.

The doctors' verdict was that he probably would never play ball again. The shattered arm became twisted and paralyzed. Even after several years of therapy under the direction of specialists, it was not straight. Still, Leo refused to be discouraged. His parents continued to seek out doctors and to try new treatments. One of the treatments prescribed was to have Leo carry pails loaded with sand and heavy rocks for hours at a time. Gradually, the arm straightened. But Hartnett couldn't play baseball for seven years after he suffered the injury.

When he was in his teens, Leo attended Dean Academy, where he played the outfield. He did not actually become a catcher until he was forced by economic circumstances in his family to leave school and go to work in the mill. With the Millville Blue Jays, he began to develop as a catcher and attract notice. In those days, industrial semi-pro leagues dotted the countryside and drew large crowds from the surrounding towns.

In 1920, Leo decided to move into faster company. He went to Worcester, where he got a job with the American Steel and Wire Company and, of course, played for the company baseball team. On weekends, he played for yet another team in nearby Uxbridge. By now, a procession of major-league scouts began to approach him. Jess Burkett, representing the New York Yankees, invited him for a tryout. John McGraw, the fiery leader of the New York Giants and a friend of Leo's father was also interested. But McGraw ultimately decided that Leo's hands were too small for him ever to become a major-league catcher.

The Worcester team in the Eastern League finally signed Hartnett to a professional contract. He caught 100 games for them in 1921, hitting .264. Though he wasn't aware of it at the time, the big leagues were fast closing in on him. One day, midway through the season, Leo found himself short of meal money and asked manager Jack Mack for a loan of a few dollars. "I'll return it to you on payday," he promised.

Mack took out five dollars and handed it to Hartnett, then said cryptically, "And don't forget to send me some postcards next spring from California."

Puzzled and slightly alarmed, Hartnett asked, "What do you mean . . . California?"

"Oh, nothing," replied Mack, "except that I've just sold you to the Chicago Cubs. You'll be in California next spring, all right."

When the story finally became unraveled, Hartnett learned that Jack Doyle, a scout for the Cubs, had come to see him play one day. Doyle liked what he saw and strongly urged the Cubs to buy Leo's contract.

Doyle explained years later why Hartnett attracted him. An old-time Baltimore Oriole from baseball's rough-and-tumble days, Doyle always insisted he could spot a ballplayer by the kind of face he had. "Hartnett had a strong puss," Doyle said.

Doyle's instinct, unscientific as it may have been, proved to be correct. Hartnett's nineteen seasons with the Cubs remain a landmark and he is still honored as the greatest catcher in the team's history. He rounded out his big-league career to twenty years of service by playing for the Giants in 1941. Then he drifted into the minors for three more seasons before retiring as an active player at the age of forty-four. In 1955, he was elected to the Hall of Fame.

Beside his many talents as a catcher, Gabby earned the respect of the umpires because he rarely questioned their calls from behind the plate. He

As a manager, Gabby had new responsibilities. Here, he talks with Baseball Commissioner Kennesaw Landis.

just went about his job. "They're my pals," he once explained. This caused some rival managers to say that umpires occasionally tended to favor Hartnett, which, of course, wasn't true. But one day, toward the end of his career, while Gabby was catching, home-plate umpire Dolly Stark was struck by a foul tip and had to leave the game. The first-base umpire picked up Stark's equipment and began to put it on so that he could take his place behind the plate. Out of the dugout came Frank Frisch, the combative manager of the St. Louis Cardinals and an umpire-baiter of great renown.

"Never mind putting another umpire behind there," he roared. "Hartnett's done a swell job of calling 'em so far this afternoon!"

Elston Howard

Manager Casey Stengel's lined and craggy face reflected the fact that he had a crisis on his hands. In the New York Yankee camp during the spring of 1954 was a tall, young rookie of infinite promise, but one who posed a number of problems to the old professor. The yearling's name was Elston Howard. The Yankees had discovered Howard playing Negro league baseball and now he was coming from an impressive year at their Kansas City farm club. He bore the unmistakable stamp of a major-leaguer.

But Stengel's problem was where to play the young man. At Kansas City, Howard had played the outfield and had been tried at catcher for a few games. Stengel could already see that he was too slow to play the outfield. But every time Howard stepped into the batting cage and ripped savage line drives up the outfield alleys, the Yankee manager realized that he would have to find another position for him to play.

Finally, Stengel drew Howard aside one day and said, "I don't think you can make it as an out-fielder in the big leagues. So, I'm gonna send Mister Bill Dickey over to you and he is going to make a catcher out of you. Even though we have a lot of catchers here, none hits the long ball except you and Mister Berra. So, I want you to be ready for when I need you."

Howard listened and nodded agreeably. "Sure," he said, "I'll try anything. I want to play in the big leagues."

But that settled only one of Stengel's dilemmas. The Yankees were under fire in the press for never having carried a Negro player on their regular roster. Earlier, they seemed to have come up with a likely prospect in first baseman Vic Power, but he had been dispatched to the Kansas City Athletics. Now that the Yankees were converting Howard into a catcher, the cynics said that the change had really been contrived to keep him from making the team. "Ain't all this a little silly?" Stengel said angrily. "You'd think we never tried a player at another position before."

When he was in a calmer frame of mind, Stengel elaborated on his reasons for shifting Elston behind the plate. "We decided that Howard's best chance to make the major leagues was as a catcher," he said. "And I've got some news for you. I think the boy is going to be a great catcher. He's willing and eager to learn. He can throw and he can hit. With

the proper amount of experience, he can be tremendous."

Still, the critics weren't convinced. One writer
sharply attacked the Yankees, charging that they
were attempting to make Howard look bad by
switching him to an unfamiliar position. Howard,
normally a quiet man who stayed clear of contro-
versy, finally became so angered over the accusa-
tions that he spoke up. "I don't see why there has
to be all this fuss about me being changed from an
outfielder to a catcher," he said. "I like to play the
outfield better because I've had more experience
there. But if Casey Stengel thinks I've got a better
chance to make the big leagues as a catcher, then

*Manager Casey Stengel wanted Howard somewhere in the
lineup for his hitting.*

I'm willing to stick at that job, even if I have to beat out a great player like Yogi Berra."

Several days after Stengel's talk with Howard, Bill Dickey opened classes for the young man in a specialized course on becoming a big-league catcher. Dickey had molded a crude Berra into an All-Star receiver. In Howard, he had someone with even more physical ability. Howard was big and strong, an ideal specimen at 200 pounds. As Stengel had correctly pointed out, Elston could hit and he possessed a strong, accurate arm and marvelous reflexes. Dickey was there merely to refine all this raw talent.

The first weakness Dickey observed in Howard's catching was his inability to handle pitches in the dirt. "It's going to take him a little while to master the knack of handling low pitches," he said, "but he's going to get it. Aside from that, there isn't anything else he can't do pretty well right now."

Howard learned quickly. He had a good training camp with the Yankees and was farmed out to their Number 1 minor-league team at Toronto for the 1954 season. Playing both catcher and the outfield, he missed winning the batting championship by two percentage points, finishing with a .330 average, twenty-two homers and 109 runs-batted-in. Toronto won the pennant. To nobody's surprise, Howard was named the International League's Most Valuable Player.

The following spring, Stengel assessed Howard's

chances of sticking with the Yankees. "He looks good," Stengel told the sportswriters, "but I can't say he's made the team yet. But I don't see why he won't stay. He can play right field, left field and catch. But because of his power, I'd have to say he's likely to be our Number 2 catcher."

Stengel apparently was sold on Howard, but there was still some caution in his mind. He reminded the writers that bullpen catcher Ralph Houk had squandered much of his career sitting on the bench as the Number 2 man behind Berra. "Houk spent nearly five years in the Army and five more on the bench as a substitute catcher," Stengel said. "Then he was through. I don't want that to happen to Howard. I'll probably use him in right field and for pinch-hitting. In an emergency, he can go behind the plate. But it's his bat we want."

Howard made the club in 1955 and thus became the first Negro to wear Yankee flannels. But with thirty-year-old Berra at the peak of his career, Ellie scarcely got the chance to catch. Stengel used him in the outfield most of the time and put him in as a sub for Berra in the second game of doubleheaders. But it was his hitting which kept him in the lineup, and Howard rewarded Stengel by producing a .290 average in ninety-seven games. He then played all seven games of the World Series against the Dodgers in the outfield, hitting a home run the first time he came to bat.

For the next several years, Howard became a

Elston firmly grips the ball for the tag at home on Washington's Chuck Hinton.

swing man in Stengel's lineup. His bat was needed to pump power into the attack, and Casey began using him at first base against left-hand pitching in addition to playing him in the outfield. He continued to spot Ellie behind the plate whenever Berra needed a day off. Stengel did his usual double-talk whenever the subject of Howard's best position came up. "I want to keep him at catcher," he said, "because in a year or two I think he can be as great as Berra or Campanella. And even if he doesn't turn out to be that, I think he can make the grade in right field or at first base."

Ellie characteristically went along with Stengel's master plan. If he ever became dismayed over Casey's machinations, he never openly showed it.

"I just want to play," he would say. "I was always an outfielder before, so naturally, I'm more comfortable there. Catching? Well, there's Berra—and he's the best. I just want to play."

Stengel accommodated Howard's wish by seeing that he played nearly every day. Ellie's appearances behind the plate were infrequent, and while he was making excellent progress as a receiver, these efforts were for the most part obscured. But they were not lost on Stengel. "You've noticed I've had him in there catching different pitchers lately," Stengel told his writers one day. "He caught Don Larsen last night for the first time in I don't know how long. And as I've said, he's becoming the finest catcher in the league. We're fortunate to have two men like him and Berra to make our catching the best anybody's got."

Still, Howard's hitting overshadowed everything else he did. After compiling modest averages of .262 and .253 in 1956 and 1957, he tore loose in 1958 with a mark of .314. For a while, he was in the race for the batting title as his average climbed to .342 in August.

That same year the Yankees stormed to their fourth pennant in a row, and Howard was singled out for making the key defensive play of the World Series—as an outfielder rather than a catcher. In the fifth game, the Milwaukee Braves, who had won the National League flag, held a 3-1 edge in games over the Yankees. They needed one more victory to become world champions. Going into the sixth inning, the Braves trailed, 1-0. Bill Bruton singled for Milwaukee. Then Red Schoendienst hit a fly ball into short left field. The blooper looked as if it would drop in for a hit. But Howard, playing in left, tore in to make a diving one-hand catch of the ball, and Bruton was subsequently doubled off first. Ed Mathews followed with a single which, without Howard's catch, easily would have scored Bruton with the tying run.

The Yanks won the game to extend the Series. They also won the sixth game, as Howard made a great throw to cut down Andy Pafko at the plate. Howard scored the winning run himself in the tenth inning. Then, in the seventh and deciding game, Ellie drove in what proved to be the clinching run when he singled up the middle to score Berra from second base. The New York Chapter of the Baseball Writers Association of America voted him the Babe Ruth Award as the outstanding player in the World Series.

The cheering had scarcely died down when Casey Stengel made a significant decision. "I gotta find a place in the lineup for this fellow Howard," he said. "It's only justice. He earned it. He's a good hitter. He has wonderful spirit. He's got a lotta talent." Stengel didn't say it in so many words, but he was heralding the arrival of Howard as Berra's successor as Number 1 Yankee catcher.

When the writers went to Ellie for his reaction,

he said, "I've got to tell you I like catching best now. But I don't like anything so good I won't pick up a fielder's glove when I see left field beside my name on the lineup card."

As usual, he was being the team man, placing the needs of the ballclub ahead of his own interests. But when he was pressed even further on the subject of taking over as catcher, he declared, "There's room for both YYogi and me on this ballclub. We can use his bat, all right, but I'd like to see him in the outfield. I want to play all the time, but I prefer catching to any other position."

For the 1959 season, the Yankees rewarded Howard with a whopping raise, jumping his salary from $17,000 to an estimated $25,000 a year. If he hadn't felt secure in his Yankee uniform before, he had

A polished catcher later in his career, Howard prevents Detroit's Al Kaline from scoring.

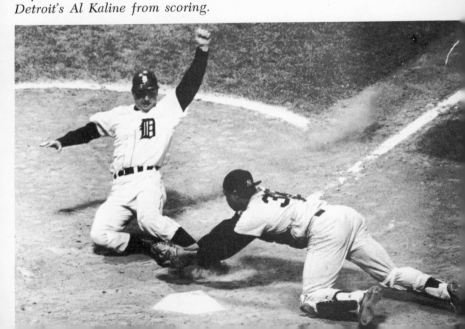

every reason to do so now. He was a big man among the Yankees now—in fact, one of the biggest.

Though Berra continued to catch more often than Howard, Yogi was slowing down. He was going on thirty-four now. Putting on the mask and pads every day and crouching down behind the plate became more and more of a burden to him. To save the wear and tear on Berra's legs, Stengel began using him in the outfield and let Howard do the catching. As a result, Ellie had his busiest campaign as a Yankee, leading the club in games played with 125. He turned in another solid year at bat with a .273 average, eighteen homers and seventy-three runs-batted-in.

In 1960, Howard was installed as the regular catcher. He had proved his right to the job to everyone. The pitchers now showed the same faith in him as they had in Berra, and Stengel trusted his judgment. Howard's confidence soared. He was sure on pop fouls and steady as a rock on plays to the plate. Baserunners feared his deadly accurate arm and rarely took chances against it. The only drawback to an otherwise fine season was a .245 batting average, Ellie's poorest mark since joining the Yankees.

Determined to bring his average back up where it belonged, Howard tried to analyze what he had been doing wrong. He decided he had been swinging too hard, going for home runs rather than base hits. "I'm going to have a good year," he promised.

"I'm going to try to hit .300. No more swinging for the fences. I want a good average."

Ellie found conditions most favorable for a resurgence when he reported for spring training the following March. For one thing, Ralph Houk was the new manager, having taken over upon Stengel's retirement. For another, Wally Moses was hired as a batting instructor, and he immediately went to work on cutting down Howard's swing and getting him to hit the ball through the middle more. "I owe a big chunk of thanks to Wally," Ellie said. "He found the cure. We decided I ought to close my stance. I'm doing that now, and that means I'm not taking my eye off the ball with those wild swings."

But mostly, Howard's return to form was due to the changed atmosphere created by Houk. Ellie was no longer asked to shift from the outfield to first base and then to catcher. Unlike Stengel, who delighted in platooning his players, Houk preferred to find the right man for the right job and keep him there permanently. He made it clear to Howard from the start that he was his catcher, period. "He's helped me. He's helped me plenty," Howard said, nodding in Houk's direction one day. "He's a quiet man and he talks things over with you. If he's got something to say, he tells you nice and quiet-like, and the next thing you know, you're talking it over."

With his new batting style, Ellie got off to a fast start in 1961. He was up among the hitting leaders all season, and in August his average climbed to

Elston's ability to play more than one position made him an instant star. Here, as a leftfielder, he makes a dramatic catch in the 1958 World Series.

.370. He had a real chance to win the batting title. Under normal circumstances, Howard's torrid pace would have dominated the sports pages. But another dramatic series of events completely overshadowed it. Roger Maris was pursuing the shadow of Babe Ruth with a phenomenal barrage of home runs, and Mickey Mantle was close at his heels. Both were attempting to top the sixty homers Ruth had hit in 1927.

Howard was almost gratified not to be in the limelight. When a reporter asked him if he felt the tension, he replied, "Not me. I'm just going along. Thank heaven for that home-run race. Everybody is concentrating on Mickey and Roger and leaving me alone. I have no worries."

But in the end, he did. While Maris established a new season high for homers with sixty-one, Ellie lost out in his bid to win the batting championship. He wound up with a mark of .348, including twenty-one homers and seventy-seven RBI's. But even if he had compiled the highest average in the league, he wouldn't have been eligible for the crown. He hadn't come to bat the required minimum number of times. Ironically, he had missed games only because he was a catcher. Though Ellie was a workhorse behind the plate, he did need an occasional day off—as all catchers do—and these rests deprived him of the necessary at-bats.

Typically, he took the outcome in philosophical fashion. "I have the best year of my life and I have to pick *that* season," he said, referring to Maris' home-run exploits.

Just two years later, however, Howard reached the milestone of his own career when he was honored as the American League's Most Valuable Player. Both Mantle and Maris were out of the lineup for considerable periods of time with injuries, and Ellie took over as the team leader. He caught 135 games and batted .287 with twenty-eight homers and eighty-five RBI's. For the third year in a row, he led all American League catchers in fielding with a .998 percentage, committing only two errors. He also played in his fourth consecutive All-Star Game. More importantly, he held the Yankee pitching staff together, enabling the club to capture another pennant.

Howard thus became the first Negro ever to win the MVP award in the American League, and the significance of the honor was lost neither on himself nor on his family. "It means so much now," explained his wife, Arlene, "because it is the period of the American Negro revolution. It makes me proud, him being the first. I tried to explain it to Elston, Jr., what it meant if his father got the award. The older boys in school made it sound very big to him and they kept telling him his father should get it. He asked me, 'What's the MVP?' I told him it's like winning the Nobel Prize. Only, it's the Nobel Prize of baseball."

There was a time in his life when Elston Gene Howard might have considered the possibility of winning the Nobel Prize for medicine. He started out wanting to be a doctor. He was born in St. Louis, Missouri, on February 23, 1929, the only child of Wayman Hill and Emmaline Howard. His father, who was a close friend of the famed Negro botanist, George Washington Carver, was a high school principal and his mother was a college-educated dietician. But as Elston grew up and began playing ball in a segregated neighborhood, he concentrated his interest on sports.

By the time he was a student at Vashon High School in St. Louis, he was an outstanding all-around athlete. He was an end on the football team, a shot-putter on the track team, a forward in basketball and a .500 hitter in baseball. Yielding to his mother's wishes, Elston decided to try to be a doctor. But the dream passed quickly when he was offered $600 a month to play baseball for the Kansas City Monarchs of the Negro League.

"As I was about to be graduated from Vashon, I had twenty-one offers," Ellie recalled years later. "Twenty were from colleges ready to give me a scholarship. One was from the Kansas City Monarchs. I sat down and doped out my course in life. There were factors which did not concern white boys. If I went to college, I would be faced, in four years, with the necessity of deciding how I would make my living. Would I still be wanted by the Monarchs? Would I have any appeal to the major-league clubs? I decided to grab what lay right under my nose and sign with the Monarchs."

Shortly after he signed with the Monarchs, Ellie heard that Jackie Robinson had been signed to play for the Montreal Royals, the top farm team of the Brooklyn Dodgers. That meant that organized baseball had opened the doors to black players, and Ellie saw his own horizons broadening. "Robinson's success induced me to drop any notion of going on to college," he said. "I never had cause to regret my decision."

Years later, Howard was to say, "Education was an important thing in my home. I didn't go to college because I turned to baseball, but I want my kids to get a college education."

He provided for that contingency by continuing to perform as one of the top stars in the game for several years after his coveted MVP award. In 1964, he moved into the $55,000 class, as his Yankee bosses gave him a whopping raise. He batted .313 and helped the club to another pennant. "I worked hard at catching," he said, "and I figure if I can do the job back there, I can make a better living there than anywhere else."

Howard had a couple of more good seasons left

Elston and Manager Ralph Houk discuss strategy with a Yankee pitcher. Houk later hired Elston as a coach.

in him, but his youth was quickly deserting him. By the 1967 season, the thirty-eight-year-old catcher could no longer take the rigors of day-in, day-out play, and in August, the Yankees traded him to the Boston Red Sox. The move gave Ellie one more chance to play for a pennant winner. The Red Sox had no one else they could rely on behind the plate, and it was Howard who helped guide an erratic and youthful pitching staff into the World Series against the St. Louis Cardinals. He came back for the 1968 campaign, but his playing days were clearly at an end and he announced his retirement as an active player when the season was over.

Ahead of him lay a new career as a coach with the Yankees and the hope of achieving his long-standing dream of becoming major-league baseball's first Negro manager. Whether or not he would make it, he could still look back on a career in which pride and determination had taken him so far. "I realized from the start," he once said, "that I was second string to Yogi, who is a cinch to be elected to the Hall of Fame someday. When I broke in, Yogi and Campanella were the best there were. Thank God, I was able to play more than one position."

Ernie Lombardi

Before a Cincinnati-Chicago game in 1934, two big men stood posing side by side for a photographer. The taller of the two was the young catcher of the Cincinnati Reds, Ernie Lombardi, a powerfully built man with an open, homely face and an oversized nose. The other man, who was older and heavier-set, with a ruddy complexion and a salty glint in his eyes, was Gabby Hartnett of the Cubs, the leading catcher in the National League.

As the photographer snapped the shutter, he said to Lombardi, "Schnozz, you're going to be the next great catcher in this league."

And Hartnett snorted, "I'm not ready to relinquish it yet."

Though Ernie Lombardi was not destined to succeed Gabby Hartnett as the league's Number 1 catcher, he was good enough to take his place among the best ever to play the game. During his playing career he won two batting titles and a Most Valuable Player award, and caught two memorable

Lombardi, left, and Hartnett, right. Who's Number One?

no-hitters. Sometimes, though, his catching talents were obscured by his more conspicuous traits. At a height of 6 feet 3 inches and weight of 230 pounds, he looked ponderous and ungainly. In addition, he probably was the slowest running ballplayer of his time. But he was a feared hitter, who gripped his bat in an unusual manner. And always there was that nose which dominated his face and often sidetracked writers from his true baseball skills. He was widely kidded about the nose, but he enjoyed most of the kidding and even responded with a good-natured, folksy humor of his own.

"They first began kidding me about the nose and calling me 'Schnozz' back in the Coast League," he once said. "But the funny thing was, I didn't get too much razzing from the bench jockeys. Mostly, it came from the fans."

One day during his brief stay in Brooklyn, someone brought entertainer Jimmy Durante to Ebbets Field to meet Lombardi. Durante had a famous "schnozzola" of his own. "They brought him into the clubhouse and took a picture of us together, nose to nose," Lombardi recalled. Durante summed up the situation when he observed, "Lom's is bigger, but mine is more educated."

Lombardi was both a product and a symbol of the time in which he played. Born six years before the start of World War I, on April 6, 1908, he grew up in Oakland, California. His father, Dominic, ran a small grocery store. When Ernie was old enough, he helped out behind the counter. But even before that, he loomed as a large figure on the sandlot ballfields of Oakland. He played most of his baseball in Bay View Park, where as many as 150 youngsters would turn out every day. (Years later, the park was renamed Raimondi Field and Ernie noted sadly that scarcely anyone goes there any more to play baseball.)

Probably because of his height, Ernie was first stationed in the outfield. When he was twelve years old, he played for a semipro team, Ravoli's Meat Market, which was sponsored by a local butcher who even furnished the players with uniforms. One day Manager Al Clark, who liked the way Ernie threw the ball, came up to him and said, "From now on, you catch." After that, Ernie was resigned to a life with the mask and pads.

There was no high school ball for the large Italian youth after he finished grammar school. Instead he went to work in his father's store. But he continued to play semipro ball into his late teens. During that period a scout for the Oakland Oaks of the Pacific Coast League was keeping track of him. Convinced that Ernie was a good prospect, he finally approached him and said, "How would you like to sign with us?"

Afraid that the Oaks might send him to one of their farm teams, Ernie replied, "Nothing doing. You ain't gonna ship me away from home."

But soon events in his life caused Ernie to change his mind. His father had to leave on a trip out of town, and he put Ernie in charge of the store.

"This ain't for me," Ernie told himself after a stint in the store, and he immediately contacted the Oaks to see if they were still interested in him. They were, and they signed him to a contract for the remainder of the 1926 season. He was nineteen years old.

Early in the following season, it became obvious that the pace of the Oakland Oaks was still too fast for the inexperienced receiver, so they sent Ernie to their farm club at Ogden, Utah. There, he ran into unexpected difficulties. The high altitude made his nose bleed and he began to lose weight. But his bat was ricocheting balls off the outfield fences. After he had raised his average to .398 in fifty games, the Oaks recalled him. "I don't know whether they brought me back to save my life or because I was hitting good," Ernie told a friend. "But I'm sure glad they did."

After batting .377, .366 and .370 in three seasons with Oakland, Ernie was purchased in 1930 by the Brooklyn Dodgers for $50,000 and two ball-players. The Dodger manager was Wilbert Robinson, who was affectionately called "Uncle Robbie" by his players. But Robinson was getting along in years and he had become quite irritable. He did not take an immediate liking to the big greenhorn catcher from the Coast. Al Lopez, one of the manager's favorites, did most of the catching that season, while Lombardi watched from a seat on the bench. But Lopez was a .260 hitter, while Lom was potentially capable of hitting for a higher average.

He proved it whenever he got the chance to play for the ragtag Dodgers. Hollis Thurston, a player who stammered whenever he talked, once kidded Ernie by saying. "Y-Y-Y-You c-c-can't p-p-p-play b-b-ball here. Y-Y-You h-h-hit the b-b-ball t-t-too h-h-hard."

Yet one day, Uncle Wilbie sent Ike Boone up to pinch-hit for Ernie. This rankled the young catcher's pride so much that he never forgot it. "It was

Ernie, putting a tag on Pittsburgh's Al Gionfriddo, was agile around home plate.

the only time in my life I was ever taken out for a pinch-hitter," he said.

By that time it was inevitable that Ernie would not last long in Brooklyn. After hitting .297 in seventy-three games during his one year with the Dodgers, he was traded to the Cincinnati Reds for the 1932 season. The Reds immediately made Ernie their first-string catcher, and he responded by hitting .303 in 118 games. Deacon Bill McKechnie was the manager, and Ernie's relationship with him was far better than the one he had had with Uncle Robbie. "I liked to play for Bill," Ernie recalled years later. "He was quieter than other managers. But all he had to do was look out at you over the top of his glasses and you'd know you'd done something wrong."

Ernie developed into a top-flight, all-around catcher with the Reds. Despite his great size he had agility behind home plate, and he got under pop fouls well. He had a strong and accurate throwing arm and runners rarely took chances against him. As for his ability to block home plate, there weren't many players big enough or tough enough to try crashing through him. "My only weakness," he used to say, "was my lack of speed. I couldn't move as fast as Rollie Hemsley or Mickey Cochrane."

He was kidded about his lack of speed almost as frequently as he was about his nose. But he wasn't

Lombardi wasn't baseball's most graceful baserunner. But he still managed to hit for high averages.

above telling stories about himself just to prove how
slow he really was. "In Cincinnati once," he said,
"I hit the left-field wall and they threw me out at
first base." Then he broke into a roaring laugh. But
what Ernie modestly neglected to tell his listener
was that they were able to throw him out partly
because he had hit the ball so hard. Ernie's hard
smash reached the outfielder sooner and enabled
the fielder to return it quicker.

On another occasion, Lom stole second base
against the Dodgers in full view of a packed house
at Ebbets Field. He had singled off Kirby Higbe.
Then, with the next batter at the plate, he headed
for second base. Dodger catcher Mickey Owen instinctively drew back his arm to throw, but when
he looked down to second, he saw the bag was va-
cant. Shortstop Pee Wee Reese and second baseman Billy Herman were so startled that neither one
of them moved for the base. As Ernie laughingly
explained later, "They couldn't move when I stole.
I was just too fast for them."

As sound a catcher as he was, Lombardi won his
reputation largely on his fearsome hitting. Though
he was never to hit more than twenty homers in a
single season, he made good contact with the ball
and he could hit for average. He lost countless doubles and triples, however, because of his inability
to run fast. But what drew special attention to his
hitting was the way Ernie held his bat. He inter-
locked the pinky finger on his right hand with the

index finger on his left hand, in very much the same manner that a golfer grips a club. Why did he hold the bat that way? Because once, while he was playing for Oakland, he got hit on his little finger with a foul tip. A blister formed which hurt when he gripped the bat. So one day he decided to try linking it with his left hand. He found the new style comfortable so kept on hitting that way.

Obviously, the unique style didn't hinder his batting form. During his ten seasons with the Reds, Ernie hit better than .300 seven times. Between 1935 and 1938, he compiled such impressive averages as .343, .333, .334 and .342. The latter figure won him a batting title. Despite the fact that the Reds did not win the pennant that year, he was voted the National League's Most Valuable Player.

The Reds of the late 1930s provided Ernie with some of the best pitchers in the game to catch. Among them were Bucky Walters, Paul Derringer and Johnny Vander Meer. Referring to Walters and Derringer, he said, "You could sit in a rocking chair and catch them guys." Then, shifting to Vander Meer, a hard-throwing but erratic left-hander, he said, "Vandy was real hard to catch because he was so wild. You never knew where the ball was going to end up when he was pitching. When you caught Vandy for nine innings, you knew you were in a game. All you'd want to do after that was go home to bed."

In 1938, Vander Meer became the only pitcher

ever to hurl consecutive no-hitters. Lombardi was the catcher in both games. On June 11th, Vander Meer no-hit the Braves, 3-0. Four days later, against Ernie's old club, the Dodgers, in a game inaugurating night baseball at Ebbets Field, Vander Meer tossed his second consecutive no-hitter, winning, 6-0.

After the game, Lombardi revealed he had signaled for Vander Meer's fastball far more often than for his curve. "That's because I had more of a chance to catch the fastball than the curve," he said. "With the curve, he might bounce it in the dirt." Lombardi also elaborated on the eternal catcher-pitcher struggle. "You call the pitches as long as they're rookies," he said. "Then, they smarten up and like to call their own game. That's

Throughout his career, catcher Lombardi was teamed with outstanding pitchers. Here, he is flanked by Paul Derringer and Bucky Walters.

when they kind of shake you off. I let them do it if they wanted to."

Of the two key plays in Vander Meer's second no-hitter, one involved Lombardi. The Dodgers were at bat and had runners on first and third with one out. The next Dodger batter hit a smash to third baseman Lew Riggs. A double play seemed risky, so Riggs decided to go for the sure out at home and preserve Vandy's shutout. He fired the ball to Lombardi, who planted the tag on the runner. Vandy then got the next batter. With two down in the ninth, Leo Durocher hit a blooper to center that looked as if it might drop in for the first hit, but centerfielder Harry Craft tore in and made the catch for the final out.

In 1939, Lombardi finally got a chance to play in his first World Series. He batted .287 in 130 games, then collected three hits in the Series against the Yankees. He earned $17,000 for the season, then picked up an additional $5,000 as his World Series share. It was the best year he ever had financially. Looking back from the vantage point of the 1960s he said, "I guess in today's market I'd be worth three times that amount."

The era in which Lombardi played ball was one of the most colorful the game has ever known, though it also had its dismal side. It was the time of the Great Depression in the Thirties with mass unemployment. People had very little money to spend on entertainment. The price of a bleacher seat was only fifty cents, yet fans were hard-pressed to come up with even that amount. "Crowds were so scarce in those days," Lombardi recalled, "that we used to call off a Wednesday game and move it to Sunday so we could play a doubleheader and get maybe four thousand people into the ballpark. We did it so often that we'd find we'd have ten days off at the end of the season."

Lombardi played in another World Series in 1940, after hitting .319 in 109 games. And he remained with the Reds through the 1941 season. But he and General Manager Warren Giles weren't getting along, and a trade appeared imminent. Ernie hoped to be sent to the New York Giants. But in 1942, Giles sold him to the Boston Braves. He was forced to take a $6,000 cut in salary.

Perhaps as a measure of revenge, Lombardi had a banner year in 1942, winning his second batting crown with an average of .330. During a Reds-Braves game that season, Ray Lamanno, the new Cincinnati catcher, told Lombardi, "Man, you're driving McKechnie crazy with the way you're hitting. He's pulling his hair out."

After one year in Boston, Ernie finally got his wish and was traded to the Giants. He was thirty-five years old now, but he still had plenty of good baseball left in him. He caught the superb Carl Hubbell and Hal Schumacher, among others, and his bat rattled out averages of .305, .255, .307 and .290 in his four years in New York. Pitcher Bill

Voiselle became his roommate on road trips. This was noteworthy because Lombardi rarely ever had a roommate in his long years in the National League. "Nobody would room with me," he used to complain. "They said I snored too much." When a writer asked Voiselle how he managed to put up with Lombardi's snoring, he replied, "I've got bad ears. I can't hear him."

Lombardi retired after the 1946 season with a lifetime batting average of .307. He dropped out of baseball and worked at a variety of jobs. But baseball was still in his blood, and he returned to the ballpark frequently, visiting his old friends in the press box and dugouts and participating in old-timers' games. But that wasn't enough. Lombardi longed to be a part of the game again, to be around the ballplayers and writers with whom he had spent so many years.

When the Giants moved to San Francisco in 1958, Ernie called up his old friend from Oakland, Bill Rigney, who now was managing the team, and asked for a job. Rigney promised to help. The Giants hired Lombardi as the custodian of their press box. He was still there during the 1969 season. Big and friendly as ever, Lombardi loves to swap stories and reminisce about an era of baseball that he'll never forget.

Tim McCarver

The Cardinal pitcher took his stretch, looked back over his shoulder at the runner leading off first, then fired to the plate. The ball came in low, bounced in the dirt and caromed off the catcher's shin-guards. The runner on first bolted for second base. In a flash, Tim McCarver, the Cardinal catcher, whipped off his mask, pounced on the ball and gunned it to second. He was just in time to catch the speeding runner.

"That McCarver is a bulldog," said Bill Dickey. "Look at him behind that plate. He knows what he's doing every minute."

The late Johnny Keane, the Cardinal manager who gave McCarver his start as a rookie receiver, said, "Tim is a throwback. He's not afraid of anything. He blocks that plate like it belongs to him."

When he said that Tim McCarver was a throwback, Keane meant that the young player reminded fans of some of the old-time catchers who were fiery and aggressive and took charge of things. He was thinking of such catchers as Mickey Cochrane, Gabby Hartnett, and Bill Delancey, the former Cardinal. McCarver is a present-day model of the tough old catchers of the 1930s.

Tim became the Cardinals' regular catcher in 1963, when he was just a twenty-two-year-old rookie. Most veteran ballplayers would have resented someone that young taking over. Others would have ignored him. But McCarver was not to be resented or ignored. He proved himself immediately to the older players. He showed them that he could catch. More important, he showed them that he could lead.

Dick Groat, a shortstop who had been in the National League ten years before McCarver first appeared in the majors, was impressed right from the start.

"Man, I can't say enough about that kid," Groat said of his young teammate. "I've never seen a guy take over the way he did. He is the best-looking young catcher I've seen since I've been in baseball."

Tim joined the Cards for their 1963 spring training. He was fresh from a year at Atlanta, then a minor-league club, where he had hit .275 and led all International League catchers in putouts. As soon as he put on his catching gear at St. Petersburg, it was obvious to nearly everyone in camp that the Cards had found their regular catcher. In 1962 the job had been held by Gene Oliver, a big man who could hit but who had defensive weaknesses. When

Tim made the team, the Cardinals traded Oliver to the Braves and gave the job to McCarver.

"When we brought him from Triple A," said Johnny Keane, "we told him he was on the ball-club. He got as much out of the minors as he was going to get. There wasn't any use in sending him back. When we traded Oliver, we told Tim he was our catcher. We didn't have to worry about it. Tim knew he could do the job and he did it. He will do it this year, too, and for many years to come." Keane died a couple of years later, but he lived long enough to see his prophecy on McCarver come true.

"That was a big break for me," Tim recalled. "I had no reservations about going in there. That's what I trained for."

Apart from his unrestrained self-confidence, Mc-Carver had other more tangible assets. As a receiver, he came equipped with sound baseball instincts; he knew pitchers and pitching, and he had a way of transmitting his knowledge to others. Though he had only an average throwing arm, he made up for that deficiency by learning how to get his throws away quickly and accurately. He also demonstrated that he could handle the difficult knuckle-ball. And, as more than one pitcher pointed out, he didn't have the annoying habit of going out to the mound on every whim.

In one memorable game during his rookie season, Tim proved to everyone's satisfaction that he knew what he was doing. The Cardinals were playing the Milwaukee Braves and Lew Burdette, an aging right-hander who had enjoyed some great years, was on the mound for St. Louis. The game was close and when it went into the late innings, Burdette began taking more and more time between pitches. Keane, sitting on the Cardinal bench, wondered if he was tiring.

The veteran manager contemplated taking Burdette out of the game when the next good Brave hitter came to bat. But suddenly, McCarver turned his face toward the Card dugout and from behind his mask blurted out, "Hey John, don't worry. We've got this guy right here." McCarver pointed to his hip pocket.

Keane winced a little at the rookie's brashness, but he decided to leave Burdette in to pitch to the hitter. "Here he was," he recounted later, "a twenty-two-year-old equal to the occasion. I looked at McCarver and I believed him. I believed they would get him out. And they did. We won, 3-1."

McCarver carried his aggressiveness wherever he went. He not only displayed his fire as a catcher who could get something extra out of a pitcher or block the plate on a baserunner, but he also showed the same courage when he was a baserunner himself. Against the Los Angeles Dodgers in one game, he barreled so hard into catcher John Roseboro that he knocked him out of action for several weeks. Roseboro was one of the best in the business at blocking home plate. In a subsequent game, Mc-Carver did the same thing to Johnny Edwards of the Cincinnati Reds. Tim took such a battering himself on the play that his teammates were amazed to see him in the starting lineup the following day.

With all his hustle, Tim wound up catching 127 games and hitting .289. Only Milwaukee's Joe Torre outhit him among regular National League catchers. His presence in the lineup once again made contenders of the Cardinals, as they made a strong run at the Dodgers. In the closing weeks of the season, the Cards won nineteen of twenty games, and barely missed winning the pennant. In those hectic days, Tim responded well in the clutch and many of the older Cardinals said he had made the difference. "Give the credit to McCarver," said veteran first baseman Bill White. "He's been great."

By the start of the 1964 campaign, McCarver was being looked to as a leader on the Cardinals despite his youth. "You just don't find kids like this," said shortstop Dick Groat. "He was born mature. He hits the good pitchers and he doesn't strike out much. You got a man on second, you can look for Timmy to move him up because he's going to get a piece of the ball. I keep referring to him as a kid. Well, he's not. He's a mature youngster. He is twenty-two chronologically, but he's a heck of a lot older than that, baseball-wise."

As the season progressed, the Cards got into the thick of the pennant fight. Old pros such as

Groat, White and Ken Boyer were the anchormen of the team. Curt Flood and Julian Javier gave them speed, defense, and timely hitting. Bob Gibson, Ray Sadecki and Curt Simmons pitched brilliantly. But it was McCarver who provided the spark. Catching virtually every day, working double-headers, playing with big and little injuries, Tim refused to ask for a day off. He knew he was an integral part of the team and that his presence was needed in the lineup every day.

"He doesn't mind getting his uniform dirty," said teammate Bill White.

Tim caught 137 games and batted .288, as the Cardinals clinched the 1964 flag on the final day of the season. In the World Series, they were rated decided underdogs against the New York Yankees. But the Cardinals had momentum going for them.

In the first game of the Series, a big Yankee inning was cut off when leftfielder Lou Brock scooped up a single and pegged a perfect throw home to McCarver, who planted the tag on Whitey Ford. The Cards won the game, 9-5. In the fifth game, with the Series deadlocked at two games apiece, Tim came up with two men on base in the top of the tenth inning. With the score tied, 2-2, he homered for a 5-2 Cardinal victory. The Cards went on to win the Series in the seventh game. Tim

Good hitting catchers were at a premium in the 1960s. Tim McCarver was one of the best.

Tim is congratulated by teammates after his three-run homer in the tenth inning won the final game of the 1964 Series against the Yankees. (N. Y. Daily News)

wound up as the batting star of the Series by getting eleven hits in twenty-three at-bats for a .478 average.

In a little more than two seasons, the Cardinals had been transformed from a second-division team to a world champion. McCarver had as much to do with the improvement as any veteran.

Early in the 1965 season, Bill White, a mature player with a serious outlook, tried to put Tim in the proper perspective. "A lot of catchers don't want to catch doubleheaders," he said. "A lot of catchers don't want to catch, period. Catching is probably one of the easiest ways to be a second-string man and stay around the majors ten or twelve years, just playing maybe twenty-five games a year, because you just can't get good catchers. Most catchers need seven or eight years in the minors to get the mechanics." Then he looked in the direction of McCarver, who was warming up a pitcher, and shook his head in amazement. "He's young, but he's been a first-string catcher for two years."

The hazards of catching caught up to Tim in 1965. He started out by breaking a finger in spring training and missing a few games at the start of the season. Then, in August, he jammed his left thumb and missed several more games. Still, he managed to stay in the lineup often enough to wind up as the National League's top defensive catcher with a percentage of .995. At the plate he batted .276 and collected eleven home runs, the most he had ever hit.

By contrast, Tim had an injury-free year in 1966. He caught 148 games and was even more productive with his bat. He hit .274 but set new career highs with 149 hits, twelve homers, sixty-eight RBI's and established a major-league record for catchers by collecting thirteen triples. The Cardinals unloaded aging stars Groat, Boyer and White and were a team in transition during 1966. But in 1967, they climbed back on top of the National League heap, and Tim soared right along with them. He batted a cool .295, slammed fourteen homers, drove in sixty-nine runs and led all league catchers with a fielding percentage of .997. He had come into his own; at age twenty-five, he was undisputably the best catcher in the league.

He also took complete charge as the team leader and sunshine man.

In July, the Cards were well out in front of the rest of the National League by a comfortable margin and apparently headed for the pennant. But July is a hot month in St. Louis and even healthy ball-players can become run down during the long grind. One day they filed into their clubhouse at Busch Memorial Stadium before a game and Red Schoendienst, who had replaced Keane as manager in 1965, noticed they were dragging their heels. "Today, they look as tired as I've ever seen them," he told a sportswriter. "Those two games last night made it thirty-seven games in thirty-six days, and they won't have an off-day from now until September 5. But somebody will start something to shake them up. Somebody always does."

"Somebody," named Tim McCarver, stood up a few minutes later, picked up the lid of a trash can nearby and began pounding it with a baseball bat. He marched around the room pounding the lid. Meanwhile Bob Gibson got the cue and began yelling, "Get up, you Cardinals. Get up and get mad." While Gibson began yelling out the names of the players McCarver, with his rakish grin, kept on pounding the lid as though it were a bass drum.

"That's the beauty of him," an old-time Cardinal player said later in September when the Cards had

the pennant all locked up. "He keeps the rest of the
players loose in the clubhouse, gets them out of
their doldrums. But if he's funny in the locker
room, he's dead serious on the field. There's no non-
sense from him. He's the leader. He takes charge
of the ballgame from start to finish. If he goes to the
mound, it's only because he really has something
helpful to say. If he finds a pitcher isn't giving
everything he's got, Tim really gives it to him. He
gives everything of himself. He wants that much
from the rest of us. He yells at the infield to stay

A team leader, McCarver issues a vocal protest to umpire
Bill McKinley.

alert to the plays and keeps reminding them of the situation—how many outs, where the runners are, where to make the next play. That's what it means to be a catcher. That's what makes him what he is."

The Cardinals were repeaters in 1968, winning the pennant by nine games. But Tim suffered a letdown at the plate. He batted only .253 with five homers and forty-eight runs-batted-in. At times, Red Schoendienst rested him and used substitute Johnny Edwards behind the plate. Amazingly, despite his season-long slump, Tim did not let it affect his morale, nor did he stop his good-natured needling of his teammates. They, in turn, kidded him right back about his slump. But everyone knew where he would be once the World Series started— in the lineup, where his leadership and aggressiveness were needed. The Cards went down to defeat in seven games to the Detroit Tigers, but Tim won one of the games with a homer. He was still their leader.

"He's been a leader ever since he learned to talk," Tim's dad once said. Tim was born in Memphis, Tennessee, on October 16, 1941. He learned to play ball at an early age and got into his first real game in the strangest way possible. As an eight-year-old, he went to watch a game that was being played by a teenage team his father coached. When the game began, his father found the team was one man short. He beckoned to Tim in the

Tim, sliding into third base, was an unusually fine baserunner for a catcher.

grandstand and put him in right field!

In those days, Tim was a right-handed batter, but this was soon changed by—of all people—his sister, Marilyn. As one of his earliest coaches, she persuaded Tim to swing from the left side because with his good running speed it would get him down the line sooner. Besides, many of the good hitters she admired were left-handed.

By the time he reached his senior year at Christian Brothers High, Tim was a solid six-footer weighing 185 pounds. He was also as outstanding at catching footballs as baseballs. College scouts were coming around with football scholarship offers. Notre Dame thought it had Tim locked up, and Tennessee got as far as signing him to a grant-in-aid. But Tim was secretly hoping a major-league baseball team would come along with an offer—any offer.

A team finally did. The team of his choice, the Cardinals, offered him a bonus when he was seventeen and he quickly signed. It was the 1959 season and Tim was assigned to Keokuk in the Class D Midwest League. He instantly took charge of the team. In sixty-five games, he batted a crisp .360. He played so well, in fact, that the Cardinals promoted him to Rochester for the final month of the season. In seventeen games at Rochester, Tim hit .357.

The following year, he played at Memphis in front of his hometown fans and batted .347. He was proving himself as a line-drive-hitting terror who came through in the clutch and as a bulldog receiver who got the most out of his pitchers. There was no question that a team played better because of his presence on the field. A low point in Tim's career came in 1961 while he was playing for Charleston. A split finger on his throwing hand bothered both his hitting and his catching. His batting average was .229. For a while, even Tim Mc-Carver began having doubts about himself.

But these doubts faded with the passing of an-

other baseball season. Tim reported for spring training in 1962 with renewed confidence and determination. He was assigned to Atlanta in the International League, and responded by having his most
productive year in professional baseball up to that
point. He hit .275 in 122 games and collected
eleven homers and fifty-seven RBI's. Defensively,
he led International League catchers in putouts.
With Tim drum-majoring the ball club, the Crack-
ers won the Little World Series.

The education of Tim McCarver was complete.
Tim was ready to meet the challenge of the major
leagues.

After seven full years with the Cardinals, Mc-
Carver was the key figure in a trade to the Philadelphia Phillies. The Cards gave up Tim and teammates Curt Flood and Joe Hoerner for slugger
Richie Allen and infielder Cookie Rojas.

McCarver took the trade in stride. He would go
to the Phillies in 1970 and try to become a leader for
a new ballclub.

Joe Torre

The manager of the Milwaukee Braves studied the face of the swarthy young catcher and asked, "How do you feel?"

"Fine," Joe Torre said. "But I haven't had any sleep."

The twenty-year-old Torre had just reported to the Braves from their Louisville farm team. Twelve hours earlier, he had been awakened from a sound sleep in his room in an Omaha hotel and ordered to report immediately.

"We're in Cincinnati," a Braves' official said over the phone. "Catch the first plane out of there." Torre had been up half the night making flight schedules.

He spent the rest of the predawn hours shuttling from one plane to another. Then, just before noon, he checked into the Netherland-Hilton Hotel in Cincinnati. He had just enough time to deposit his bags and hop a cab to Crosley Field for the game.

Although Torre claimed to feel fine, Manager Charlie Dressen had his doubts.

"You look tired to me," he said. "It wouldn't be fair to use you in this condition. Take the rest of the afternoon off. You can make up for it tomorrow. We've got a doubleheader, and you can catch both games."

Although Dressen had faith that the rookie receiver could handle the job, he was acting out of desperation at the moment. The Braves were into the 1961 season and their regular catcher, Del Crandall, had come down with a mysterious arm ailment. His throwing arm was so sore, he could hardly lift it to comb his hair. The Braves were playing poorly without a good catcher, and Dressen knew he needed help. He had been keeping an eye on Torre's development at Louisville and noticed he was hitting .342 as well as doing a capable job of handling the pitching staff. "Get me Torre," he told the front office, and now he had him.

Torre had a full night's sleep to recover from the shock of having to break into the major leagues by catching both ends of a doubleheader. When he got to the ballpark the next day, he received a fresh jolt. He discovered that Warren Spahn was pitching the first game. Spahn was merely the game's foremost left-hander at the time, a perennial twenty-game winner who was closing in on the magic figure of 300 lifetime victories. Needless to say, the young catcher was in awe of his first big-league assignment.

Spahn quickly put Torre at his ease. "You call

The Braves took a chance on young Joe Torre. It paid off.

your own game," the pitcher said. "If I don't agree, I'll shake you off."

The first few innings were a nightmare to Torre. He was trying to concentrate on calling the right pitches for Spahn. He knew the veteran still had plenty of hop on his fastball, superb control and a wicked curve. He didn't want to do anything that might upset his rhythm. He felt uncomfortable in his catcher's crouch. His equipment seemed to pinch him in the wrong places.

Then, suddenly, the Cincinnati batter, Wally Post, hit a pop foul directly overhead. Instinctively, Torre ripped off his mask and got under the ball. After a seeming eternity of waiting, the ball plopped into his mitt. He breathed a hugh sigh of relief that he had come through his first "crisis."

"I wasn't very good on pop-ups then," Joe said, "and I could feel my knees knock. But I got the mask off, saw the ball real well, and caught it. I knew then I was okay. I was in the big leagues."

In the doubleheader, Joe homered, doubled and singled. He was equally impressive behind the plate. The Reds, doing what any team would against a rookie catcher, decided to test him early in the game. They ran on him whenever they could. They paid a price for it, however, because Joe threw out Vada Pinson, Frank Robinson and Eddie Kasko when they attempted to steal. In the second game, Torre saved a victory for the Braves when he tagged Pinson out at the plate on a heads-up play that would have brought credit to a veteran. Pinson was racing the ball home, and the throw came in slightly off line. But Joe grabbed it, whirled and tagged Pinson so hard the Cincinnati outfielder went sprawling to the ground.

The rest of the league also quickly learned that Torre wasn't an ordinary rookie. He wasn't going to be cowed in the presence of illustrious big-leaguers. He knew he had to be just as tough and aggressive as everyone else, and he decided to make this known as early as possible.

Later that season, Spahn was going for his 300th win with Torre behind the plate. The veteran pitcher, who had won his first game as a professional before Torre was born, and the rookie receiver enjoyed a fine rapport. Joe was rapidly maturing as a catcher and as a major-leaguer, and Spahn trusted his judgment on pitches. Joe was at his best guiding Spahn through this most crucial game of his career. He even helped Spahn to an early lead when he doubled in the fifth inning and eventually came around to score. Then, in the ninth, with the Braves leading the Cubs, 2-1, Spahn was down to his final out.

Torre signaled for a screwball. But Spahn shook him off for the first and only time during the game. He wanted the fastball. So Spahn got the hitter on a fly to right and walked off the field with his 300th career victory.

Later, Spahn paid tribute to Torre's catching. "Even from the first day," Spahn said, "you knew this was an exceptional kid. You forgot how young he was. He thinks very well. He catches for the pitcher—not for himself. He's not afraid to call for the change-up or the screwball with runners on. He's not like some catchers who are defensive. They like the fastball all the time, so they can defend themselves against baserunners. Joe knows the object of the game is to get the hitter out. If he guesses wrong, he's ready to take the blame."

Joe spent the rest of the 1961 season filling in for Crandall, and wound up batting .278, collecting ten homers and forty-two runs-batted-in in 113 games. Though some of his inexperience behind the plate showed through occasionally, his debut was nevertheless remarkable for a rookie who had just turned twenty-one and was playing in only his second year of professional ball. The sportswriters demonstrated how highly they regarded him when they voted him second to Chicago's Billy Williams for "Rookie of the Year" honors.

"Joe Torre," said Crandall, "is the finest young catcher I have seen come up to the big leagues since I've been here."

Torre was no ordinary rookie on several counts. For one thing, he didn't look like a rookie. Already, he was a muscle-hard 210-pounder with dark features accentuated by thick, bushy eyebrows that made him look older. For another, he didn't act like a rookie. He had an air of poise and self-assurance that showed he belonged. Joe's confidence in himself went back to his boyhood when he decided that someday he would play ball in the major leagues. But if Joe Torre himself never doubted that he would make the majors, there was a time when no one else shared his confidence.

Joe grew up in a world of brick and asphalt in Brooklyn, the most populated of the five boroughs that make up New York City. His neighborhood was an orderly one. But there were none of the rural advantages of Willie Mays' hometown in Alabama or Mickey Mantle's birthplace in Oklahoma, where a young player could throw a baseball into the air and put home plate wherever it came down. Joe's community was a middle-class neighborhood of comfortable brick homes. His father supported the family on the salary of a New York City policeman.

Joe can't remember when he played his first game of ball. His personal sandlot was a city playground known as Marine Park, which was conveniently located on the corner of his block. "We always had a game going," he recalled. "My older brothers, Rocco and Frank, were always playing ball. So I came to it naturally."

When Frank was nine years older, and already regarded as a good first-base prospect, Joe was barely out of his knee pants. In 1951, the Braves signed Frank and sent him to their farm club at Denver. A couple of months later, ten-year-old Joe was permitted to visit him with an aunt. It turned out to be the peak experience of his boyhood. The Denver players quickly adopted the likable youngster, outfitted him with a uniform and let him practice with them before their games. When he returned to Brooklyn, Joe was quite a celebrity around Marine Park.

Not all of the notoriety came from the fact that he had a brother playing professional ball. Joe was drawing a lot of attention as one of the best young players in the neighborhood. He hit some of the longest home runs anyone had seen at Marine Park. By the time he reached the age of twelve, Joe had

Joe, when he was young, with his brother, Frank. The Braves laughed at Joe because of his size. (N. Y. Daily News)

formed his own team and even managed to wangle a few spare uniforms from a team of older boys called the Cadets. Eventually, he was good enough to play for the Cadets and, later on, he graduated to the Brooklyn Parade Grounds league, which had cradled many other big-league players.

The scouts were coming around now to see if what they heard about Joe's hitting was true. They were impressed by the distance he could hit a baseball, but they were put off by the diameter of his beltline. Joe had taken an early fancy for eating, and by the time he reached fifteen, he weighed an almost unbelievable 240 pounds. The scouts turned away. "Where can you play a kid that fat?" they reported to their clubs. "He can't move fast enough."

Even Joe's father, who had become a Braves' scout when Frank signed, couldn't consider him as a prospect. "I wanted to sign him," he said, "but he always kept his feet under the table."

One day, after Frank had begun playing in the majors, the Braves were in town for a series with the Dodgers at Ebbets Field. Joe accompanied Frank to the ballpark to take in some of the early workout. Frank brought him into the clubhouse and introduced him to the other Milwaukee players. "This is my little big brother," he said.

Warren Spahn stared at Joe and said, "Boy, are you fat."

The other players laughed and Joe tried to hide his embarrassment as well as he could. Later, he worked out with the team and even hit one into the left-field seats. But the players' laughter stayed in his ears. Joe decided if he ever was going to join Frank in the majors, he was going to have to do something about his weight. He started by cutting down on the chocolate sodas he loved so much and passing up second helpings of spaghetti and meatballs.

Before this embarrassing episode, Joe had played mostly first and third base. He was too big and slow for the outfield or second or shortstop. Besides, his hitting, not his fielding, kept him in the lineup. He was the star hitter of his high school team, St. Francis Prep, and when he graduated, he was offered a scholarship to play baseball at St.

John's University. But Joe wasn't interested in going to college. He was intent on making it to the big leagues, even if the scouts were shunning him.

Joe's father and brother, among others, had been urging him all along to try catching. Joe had been opposed to the idea. But after he turned eighteen, he began to give it serious thought. This might be the opening he was looking for. Although he was big and beefy—his weight was still up to approximately 225 pounds—he was not ungainly. He had powerful wrists and hands and a strong throwing arm. He went to the manager of the local Cadet team, a man named Jim McElroy, and asked for the chance to catch.

"Sure," said McElroy, "but you'll have to share the job."

"That's okay with me," Joe said.

An incredible thing happened the first time Joe put on the pads, chest protector and mask and squatted down behind the plate in a catcher's crouch. He immediately became the personification of a catcher. Honey Russell, a local scout for the Braves who had been keeping an eye on Joe for years and had rejected him because of his heft, now looked on in astonishment.

"Now, this is going to be hard to believe," Russell said, "but the first time he went behind the bat, he looked as though he had been there all his life. I couldn't believe it. He was a natural."

Almost before Russell's eyes, Torre was transformed into a solid major-league catching prospect. Gradually, he began to pare off his weight, too. Catching helped him sweat off the excess pounds, and he became stronger and harder through his chest and shoulders. The streamlining job even made him a stronger hitter, since he got around on the ball quicker. Russell now realized he would have to move fast if he was to sign Joe for the Braves. Other scouts were beginning to show fresh interest in him. One night Russell paid a visit to the Torre home in Brooklyn. After a lengthy haggling session, in which the entire family participated, he got Joe's signature on a $26,000 bonus contract.

Joe was shipped to the Braves' Class C minor-league club at Eau Claire, Wisconsin, for the 1960 season, and he proceeded to tear Northern League pitching apart. He batted .344 to win the batting title, and collected sixteen homers and seventy-four RBI's. Behind the plate, he committed so few errors that he led the league's catchers in fielding. But he was still raw defensively by professional standards. One of his weaknesses was a habit of blinking on high inside pitches where the batter would swing and miss. To correct this fault, his manager, Bill Steinke, used to steal up on Joe in the locker room and suddenly poke his hand out in front of his face. Joe soon learned not to blink.

As soon as the Northern League season was concluded, Joe was brought up by the Braves in late September. He broke into a couple of games, and in his first at-bat against a major-league pitcher, he singled off left-hander Harvey Haddix. His good year at Eau Claire earned Joe a promotion to Louisville the following season. Actually, Steinke had told the Braves that Joe was ready to play in the majors. But Del Crandall was still going strong and everyone felt that another year in the minors would help sharpen Torre's catching. Joe had caught only a total of 119 games as a professional, and he still had things to learn. But when Crandall suddenly came down with his strange arm ailment and the Braves needed immediate help behind the plate, Joe was summoned. When he got that middle-of-the-night telephone call in Omaha, he did not realize that his minor-league seasoning had come to an end.

In 1962, Torre shared the catching job with Crandall, whose arm miseries disappeared as strangely as they had occurred. Joe got into eighty games and batted a solid .282. There was no question that he could hit big-league pitching, and the Braves knew they would have to find some position in which to play him as long as Crandall was the catcher.

The following season, the Braves' new manager, Bobby Bragan, placed Joe at first base and was pleasantly surprised to find out that he could play the position more than adequately. He was even more pleased when Joe wound up hitting .293 and increasing his home-run and RBI totals to fourteen

Joe is congratulated by teammates after a booming home run against Houston.

and seventy-one, respectively. Joe's major-league career was beginning to take off.

By the next season, Crandall had gone and Torre was installed as the Braves' regular catcher. He celebrated the move by having an extraordinary year. His .321 batting average marked the first time in nine years that a regular National League catcher had hit better than .300, and he added twenty homers and 109 RBI's to what was an All-Star year for him in every way. He was voted to the All-Star team for the first time, led the league's catchers in fielding percentage with .994 and was chosen by his teammates as the Braves' most valuable player for 1963.

Once Torre took over as first-string catcher, he needed little time to establish himself as the best receiver in the league. One high-level baseball official said that if he were going to start building a team from scratch, he would choose Torre as his first player. "You have to start with a catcher," he said, "and Torre's the best."

Another top baseball man, George Weiss of the New York Mets, offered to buy Torre's contract from the Braves for the astronomical price of $500,000. John McHale, the Braves' general manager, was bowled over by the offer, but managed to maintain his composure well enough to say, "He's not for sale—at any price."

In truth, Torre came by his high rating as an offensive catcher more than as a defensive catcher. That is, his greatest value to a team derived from what he could do with a bat in his hands. As a receiver, he was well repected, if not close to brilliant. His sharpest defensive weapon was his powerful throwing arm which kept baserunners from taking reckless chances against his team. His burly body seems to have been constructed for blocking the plate. He may never rank alongside Bill Dickey

Torre's ability to play first base, too, made him a valuable asset to the St. Louis Cardinals in 1969.

or Mickey Cochrane or Roy Campanella with his defensive skills, but this still leaves a great many catchers well behind him.

In ensuing seasons, Torre continued to pound National League hurling as though he really had something against pitchers. In 1965, he batted .291 and belted twenty-seven homers, not including the one he hit in the All-Star Game. He was named the league's outstanding catcher for the season with a fielding average of .993. In 1966, he was one of the game's leading sluggers with a .315 average, thirty-six homers and 101 RBI's. The following year, he slumped to .277 and twenty homers.

Joe went into the 1968 campaign determined to have a big year. But in April, he was struck in the face by a pitch and was hospitalized for two weeks with a fractured cheekbone. Typically, when he was hit, he refused to be carried from the field. "I wasn't going to be carried off," he said. "I never want that happening to me."

When he was able to resume playing, he came down with a sore arm and was in and out of the lineup. His average hovered around the .270 mark all year.

A month before the start of the 1969 season, the Braves traded Torre to the St. Louis Cardinals for first-baseman Orlando Cepeda. Now the Cardinals had two of the best catchers in the league in Torre and Tim McCarver. But they had no one to play first base with Cepeda gone. Since Joe had played a lot of first base when he wasn't catching, the Cards decided to play him at first. It was also felt that the switch to an easier position would help prolong Joe's career. Perhaps Joe realized better than ever the value of taking off all that excess weight years earlier. Trimmer and more agile at twenty-nine than he was five years before, he showed the Cardinals that he could make all the plays at first.

Torre's presence on the club also gave the Cardinals security behind the plate in case McCarver got hurt. As it turned out, Tim was out of the lineup for a considerable stretch toward the end of the 1969 season. Torre put the mask and pads on and returned to his original position. As he proved, he still knew how to handle himself behind the plate, and he still loved it. As he had said more than once, "I think that catching is a fantastic position to play."

Index

Page numbers in italics refer to photographs.

5220